ANCIENT HISTORY FROM THE MONUMENTS.

THE

HISTORY OF BABYLONIA.

BY THE LATE

GEORGE SMITH, Esq.,

OF THE DEPARTMENT OF ORIENTAL ANTIQUITIES, BRITISH MUSEUM.

EDITED BY

REV. A. H. SAYCE,

ASSISTANT PROFESSOR OF COMPARATIVE PHILOLOGY, OXFORD.

PUBLISHED UNDER THE DIRECTION OF
THE COMMITTEE OF GENERAL LITERATURE AND EDUCATION
APPOINTED BY THE SOCIETY FOR PROMOTING
CHRISTIAN KNOWLEDGE.

LONDON:
SOCIETY FOR PROMOTING CHRISTIAN KNOWLEDGE,
NORTHUMBERLAND AVENUE, CHARING CROSS, W.C.
43, QUEEN VICTORIA STREET, E.C.
26, ST. GEORGE'S PLACE, HYDE PARK CORNER, S.W.
BRIGHTON: 135, NORTH STREET.
NEW YORK: E. & J. B. YOUNG & CO.
1884.

.BLACK STONE CONTRACT TABLET OF MARUDUK-NADIN-AHI,

page 102.

PREFACE.

Mr. George Smith left his "History of Babylonia" in so nearly complete a state, that an editor had little more to do than to see it through the press, correct one or two errors, and make a few additions.

In the performance of this work, which has been one of mingled pain and pleasure, I have changed the author's words and spelling only where there was an obvious oversight, throwing other corrections into footnotes. My own responsibility for these, as well as for other footnotes containing additions to the text, is indicated by a capital S. I have also to take upon myself the responsibility of the Appendix upon the meaning of the proper names, as well as of the table of Babylonian kings and the larger part of the first introductory chapter, of which only the first page or two were written by Mr. Smith. Brackets mark the inserted portion. The Index is due to the kindness of Mr. Greenwood Hird.

Two expressions which will be met with in the book need a short explanation. The abbreviation W. A. I. denotes the series of volumes containing the cruciform "Inscriptions of Western Asia," published

necessary correction is far less than might have been expected. In fact, with the exception of the account of the Deluge, I have left the translations contained in the first chapter untouched, as they are substantially correct, and a more or less exact rendering of a particular word is not of such great consequence to the general reader. I have, however, revised the translation of the Deluge tablet throughout, and brought it up to the present level of knowledge. Here the subject is one which makes it of importance that the sense of every word should be given with as great exactitude as possible, while it belongs to a class of literature the obscurities of which have been in great measure cleared away by the researches of the last half dozen years.

One of the most interesting results of Mr. Rassam's excavations has been the discovery of the great temple of the Sun-god of Sippara in the mounds of Abu-Habba. The site of Sippara, the Sepharvaim of Scripture, has thus been fixed, and the cuneiform documents found there have afforded valuable aid in the reconstruction of Babylonian history and chronology. One of them informs us that an image of the deity which had been carried away by the nomad Sutu during the reign of Simmas-sipak (the son of

Irba-Sin) had been subsequently recovered by the king Nebo-bal-iddin. An inscribed stone, again, sent home by Mr. Rassam gives an account of a war with Elam in the time of Nebuchadnezzar I. (B.C. 1150). In this way, little by little, the gaps in our knowledge of Babylonian history are being filled up, but we are still a long way from having that fulness of information in regard to it that we now possess in regard to the history of the sister-kingdom of Assyria.

A. H. SAYCE.

TABLE OF CONTENTS.

List of Babylonian Kings, with their approximate dates *page* 9

CHAPTER I.—INTRODUCTION .... *page* 13

CHAPTER II.—THE MYTHICAL PERIOD.

Origin and chronology of Babylonian history—The ten antediluvian kings of Berosus—The Flood—The Garden of Eden—The Izdhubar or Nimrod legends—Discoveries in Southern Babylonia ....*page* 33

CHAPTER III.—CHALDEA, OR SOUTH BABYLONIA.

Nipur and Ur—Urukh and his buildings—The religion and civilization of Ur—Dungi—The kings of Karrak—The rise of Larsa ....*page* 69

CHAPTER IV.—UPPER BABYLONIA.

Cities of Upper Babylonia—Agu-kak-rimi—Sargon I.—Naram-Sin—Hammurabi—Babylon made the capital—The successors of Hammurabi, and the Kassite dynasty—Intercourse with Assyria—The Assyrian conquest of Babylonia ...... *page* 81

CHAPTER V.—THE ELAMITES IN BABYLONIA.

Elam or Susiana—Invasions of Babylonia by Kudur-nanhundi and Chedorlaomer—Kudur-Mabuk—Flood at Babylon—Wars between Babylon and Assyria—Nebuchadnezzar I. and Maruduk-nadin-ahi—Seven unknown kings .... *page* 96

CHAPTER VI.—THE PERIOD OF THE ASSYRIAN WARS.

Obscure kings—Nabu-pal-idina and Assur-nazir-pal—Disputed succession—Conquests of Shalmaneser—The Chaldees—Maruduk-zakir-izkur—Semiramis—The era of Nabonassar—The Babylonian campaigns of Tiglath-pileser .... *page* 106

CHAPTER VII.—MERODACH-BALADAN AND THE DESTRUCTION OF BABYLON.

Merodach-baladan, the Chaldean, conquers Babylon—Defeated by Sargon—Sargon king of Babylon for five years—Hagisa—Merodach-baladan retakes Babylon—Battle of Kisu—Belibni governor of Babylon—Assur-nadin-sum—Sennacherib's naval expedition to Nagitu—Revolt of Suzub—Elam devastated by the Assyrians—Battle of Khalule—Destruction of Babylon by Sennacherib. .... *page* 121

CHAPTER VIII.—THE RULE OF THE ASSYRIANS.

The successors of Assur-nadin-sum—Nabu-zir-napisti-esir—Babylon rebuilt by Esar-haddon—Succeeded by his son Saul-mugina—Wars with Elam—Revolt of Babylonia—Crushed by Assur-bani-pal—Saul-Mugina perishes in the flames of his palace—Nabopolassar appointed governor—He marries the daughter of Cyaxares of Media—The fall of Nineveh *page* 143

CHAPTER IX.—THE EMPIRE OF NEBUCHADNEZZAR.

Rise of the Babylonian Empire—Egypt and Media—Nebuchadnezzar, his conquests and buildings—Destruction of Jerusalem—Invasion of Egypt—Siege of Tyre—The kingdom of Lydia—Babylon adorned—Character of Nebuchadnezzar—Evil-Merodach—His murder—Nergalsharezer .... *page* 158

CHAPTER X.—THE DECLINE AND FALL OF THE BABYLONIAN EMPIRE.

Laborosoarchod—Nabonidos—Astyages and Cyrus—Inscriptions of Cyrus—Conquest of Babylon—Return of the Jews from exile—Kambyses and Smerdis—Darius Hystaspes—Revolt and capture of Babylon—Second revolt of Babylon under Arahu—Babylon taken—Decline of Babylon ....*page* 176

LIST OF BABYLONIAN KINGS, WITH THEIR APPROXIMATE DATES.

(*From Berosus and Abydenus.*)

THE MYTHICAL PERIOD—BEFORE THE DELUGE.

Alorus of Babylon, "the Shepherd of the People," for 10 sari, or 36,000 years.

Alaparus, or Alasparus (? of Pantibibla), for 3 sari, or 10,800 years.

Amelon, or Amillarus of Pantibibla, for 13 sari, or 46,800 years.

Ammenon of Chaldea (in whose time the Musarus Oannes, or Annedotus, half man and half fish, ascended from the Persian Gulf), for 12 sari, or 43,200 years.

Amegalarus, or Megalarus, or Metalarus, of Pantibibla, for 18 sari, or 64,800 years.

Daonus, or Daos, the shepherd, of Pantibibla (in whose time four double-shaped beings, named Euedokus, Eneugannus, Eneubulus, and Anementus, ascended from the sea), for 10 sari, or 36,000 years.

Euedoreskhus, or Euedorakhus, of Pantibibla (in whose time another Annedotus, called Odakon, or Ano-daphos, ascended from the sea), for 18 sari, or 64,800 years.

Amempsimus, a Chaldean of Larankha, for 10 sari, or 36,000 years.

Otiartes (Opartes), or Ardates, a Chaldean of Larankha (called Ubara-Tutu "the Slave of Sunset," of Surippak, or Suripkhu in the inscriptions), for 8 sari, or 28,800 years.

Sisithrus, or Xisuthrus, his son, for 18 sari, or 64,800 years. Kronos (Hea) ordered him to build an ark, after burying a history of Babylonia in Sippara; and the Deluge began on the 15th of the month Dæsius (May and June). Sisithrus was translated after the Deluge, but his companions returned to Chaldea and exhumed the buried records at Sippara. From the reign of Alorus to the Deluge were 120 sari, or 432,000 years.

AFTER THE DELUGE.

First Dynasty of 86 Kings for 34,080 or 33,091 years, headed by Evekhous, or Evexius, or Eutykhius (identified with Nimrod by Syncellus) for 4 neri, or 2,400 years, and his son Comosbelus, or Khomasbelus, for 4 neri and 5 sossi, or 2,700 years.

Their five next successors were:—

Porus for 35 years.
Nekhubes for 43 years
Nabius for 48 years.
Oniballus for 40 years.
Zinzerus for 46 years.

War of Titan (? Etanna), Bel, Prometheus, and Ogygus, against Kronus Building of the Tower of Babel, and dispersion of mankind.

HISTORICAL PERIOD.

Second dynasty of 8 Median kings, for 224 years, headed by Zoroaster (?).
Third dynasty of 11 kings.
Fourth dynasty of 49 Chaldean kings for 458 years.
Fifth dynasty of 9 Arabian kings for 245 years.[1]
1. Mardokentes, 45 years.
2. (Wanting.)
3. Sisimardakos, 28 years.
4. Nabius, 37 years.
5. Parannus, 40 years.
6. Nabonnabus, 25 years.

Sixth dynasty consisting of Semiramis.
Seventh dynasty of 45 Assyrian kings for 526 years.
Phulus and Nabonassar.

(From the Canon of Ptolemy.)

	B.C.
Nabonasar (Nabu-natsir), 14 years	747
Nabius (Nebo-yusapsi), 2 years	733
Chinzirus and Porus (Ucin-zir and Pul), 5 years	731
Ilulæus, or Yugæus (Yagina), 5 years	726
Mardokempadus (Merodach-Baladan), 12 years	721
Arkeanus (Sargon), 5 years	709
Hagisa, or Akises, 30 days	704
Merodach-Baladan (restored) 6 months	704
Belibus (Bel-ibni), 3 years	703
Apronadius (Assur-nadin-sum), 6 years	700
Rigebelus, 1 year	694
Mesesi-mordakus, 4 years	693
[Babylon destroyed B.C. 689].	
Interregnum, 8 years	689
Assaradinus (Essar-haddon), 13 years	681
Saosduchinus, or Sammughes (Saul-mucin, or Saul-mugina), 20 years	668
Kiniladanus (Assur-bani-pal), 22 years	648
Nabo-polassarus, 21 years	626
Nabokolasar (Nebuchadnezzar), 43 years	605
Ilouarodam (Evil-Merodach), 2 years	562
Nerikassolasar, or Neriglissor (Nergal-sarra-yutsur), 4 years	560
Laborosoarchodus, 3 months	556
Nabonidus, or Labynetus (Nabu-nahid), 17 years	556
Cyrus takes Babylon	539-8

(From the Inscriptions.)

AFTER THE DELUGE.

Mythical Period.

Etanna.
Ner.
Tammuz, Isullanu } the husbands of Istar.
Banini, with his wife Milili, and seven sons, the eldest of whom was Mimangab, 'the thunderbolt.'
Izdhubar, the son of Dannat, 'the strong woman.'

. . . . . .

.... nini.
Dimir-illat, his son.
Mul-ega-nunna.
Ane-kis.

. . . . . .

Historical Period.

Kings of Ur.

B.C. 3000—2000

Lig-Bagas, king of all Babylonia.
[Khassimir was one of his viceroys.]
Dungi, his son.

. . . . . .

Su-Agu.
Amar-Agu.
Ibil-Agu.

---

[1] This dynasty is probably to be identified with the second Cassite or Kossæan dynasty of the inscriptions. In this case the number of kings, as well as the duration of their reigns given by the copyists of Berosus, will have to be largely increased.

Viceroys.

Me-sa-Nana-calama, son of Be . . khuk, of Eridhu.

. . .

Idadu, of Eridhu.

. . .

Adi-Anu, of Zerghul.

. . .

Gudea, of Zerghul.

. . .

Enu-Anu, of Zerghul.

. . . .

Ilu-mutabil, of Diru (of a later date).

Elamite Kings in Babylonia.

Cudur-nankhundi. B.C. 2280

. . . . .

Chedorlaomer (Gen. xiv.).
Amar-pel, of Sumir (Shinar).
Arioch, of Ellasar.
Turgal, of Gutium.

. . . . .

Simti-silkhak.
Cudur-mabug, his son.

Kings of Larsa.

Nur-Rimmon.

. . . . .

Gasin . . .

. . . .

Sin-idina.

. . . . . .

Rim-Agu, or Eri-Acu (Arioch), son of Cudur-Mabug.

Kings of Karrak.

B.C. 2000—1700

Gamil-Adar (also king of Ur).

. . . .

Libit-Nana (also king of Ur).

. . . .

Ismi-Dagon (also of Ur).
Gungunnuv, his son.

. . . . .

Ili . . zat.

Kings of Erech.

Belat-sunat (a queen).
Sin-gasit.
(Perhaps they preceded the kings of Karrak).

Kings of Aganè.

Ai . . .
Amat-nim . . .
Sargon, for 45 years.
Naram-Sin, his son.
Ellat-Gula, a queen.
(Conquered by Khammuragas.)

Kings of Babylon.

'Sumu . . .
Zabû (built the temples of Istar and the Sun at Sippara).
Abil-'Sin.
'Sin- . . .

First Cassite Dynasty.

Ummikh-zirritu.
Agu-ragas, his son.
Abi . . his son.
Tassi-gurumas, his son
Agu-kak-rimi, his son.

Kings of Babylon.

Second Cassite Dynasty (probably the Arabians of Berosus) B.C. 1700—1300.

Khammuragas, cotemporary with Samsu-iluna.
Ammi-dicaga.
Curi-galzu I.
Simmas-sipak I.
Ulam-buryas.
Nazi-murudas I.
Meli-sipak I.
Burna-buryas I.
Cara-Cit.

. . . .

Saga-saltiyas.

. . . .

Murudas-sipak.

. . . .

Cara-indas . . .	about 1450
Burna-buryas II. . . .	. 1430
Cara-murudas	. 1410
Nazi-bugas	. 1400
Curi-galzu II. . . .	. 1380
Meli-sipak II. . . .	. 1350
Merodach-Baladan I. . .	. 1325
Nazi-murudas II. . .	. 1300

Assyrian Dynasty.

Tiglath-Adar . .	B.C. 1270
Rimmon- . . . bi . .	. 1230
Zamama-zacir-idin . .	. 1200

Chaldean Kings.

Nabu-cudura-yutsur (Nebuchadrezzar) 1150
Cara-buryas 1120
Merodach-nadin-akhi . . . 1100
Merodach-sapik-zirrat . . . 1097
. . . Sadua 1080

. . . . .

'Simmas-sipak, the son of Irba-Sin, reigned 17 years.
Hea-mucin-ziri, the son of Cutmar (an usurper), for 3 months.
Cassu-nadin-akhi, son of Sappai, for 6 years.

Dynasty from the Persian Gulf.

Ulbar-surci-idina, son of Bazi, for 15 years.
Nebuchadrezzar II., son of Bazi, for 2 years.
. . . Sukamuna, son of Bazi, for 3 months.
After these an Elamite for 6 years.

. . . . .

Rimmon-pal-idina.

. . . . .

Nebo-zacira-iscun.

. . . . .

Irba-Merodach.

Merodach-Baladan II., his son.

. . . . .

Rimmon-zacira-yutsur.

. . . . .

Sibir (invaded South Assyria).

. . . . .

Nebo-baladan . . . B.C. 880
Merodach-zacira-izcur . . . 853
Merodach-balasu-ikbu . . . 820

. . . . .

Nabu-natsir 747
Nabu-yusapsi 733
Ucin-ziru 731
Tiglath-Pileser (Porus) of Assyria 729
Yagina, chief of the Caldai . . 726
Merodach-Baladan III., his son . 721
Sargon of Assyria . . . 709
Merodach-Baladan restored . 704
Bel-ibni 703
Assur-nadin-sumi 700
Suzub 693
Essarhaddon of Assyria . . 681
Saul-mucinu 668
Assur-bani-pal 648
Bel-zacira-iscun 626
Nabopalassar 626
Nebuchadrezzar III. . . . 605
Amil-Merodach 562
Nergal-'sarra-yutsur . . . 560
Nabu-nahid 556
Merodach-'sarra-yutsur . . 541
Cyrus 538

HISTORY OF BABYLONIA.

CHAPTER I.

INTRODUCTION.

BABYLONIA was bounded on the north by Assyria, on the east by Elam, or Susiana, on the west by the Desert of Arabia, and on the south by Arabia and the Persian Gulf. The country is watered by the lower courses of the Euphrates and Tigris, and in fact it may be considered as entirely the gift of those streams. Babylonia is in general a long level tract of alluvial soil, which has been deposited through several thousand years at the mouths of these rivers. Through the accumulation of new ground at the points where the Tigris and Euphrates discharge themselves into the Persian Gulf, the Babylonian territory has steadily increased from age to age. In early Chaldean times the sea reached to Abu-Shahrein; in the time of Sennacherib it had receded to Bab-

Salimiti; in the days of Nebuchadnezzar the port was moved out to Teredon, and since the fall of Babylon many miles have been added to the land.

The inhabitants of Babylonia have always mainly consisted of two classes, the agricultural population and dwellers in towns on one side, and the wandering, pastoral, tent-dwelling tribes on the other. The greatest feature of the country was its agriculture, which was mainly carried on through artificial irrigation, the whole country being intersected with canals, some of them navigable and of great size, their banks in some places being from twenty to thirty feet high. The long deserted lines of mounds, which even now exist in hundreds, marking the lines of these artificial rivers, form far more remarkable objects than the ruined cities and palaces. Once these channels teemed with life and industry, and were lined with cities containing thousands of people; now they are an arid desert waste, supporting only a few wandering tribes of Arabs. Babylonia is without doubt the oldest civilized country in Asia, and even outside that continent only Egypt can rival it in this respect; but the history of Babylonia has an interest beyond that of Egypt, on account of its more intimate connection with the origin of our own civilization: Babylonia was the centre from which civilization spread into Assyria, from thence to Asia Minor and Phœnicia, from these to Greece and Rome, and from Rome to modern Europe.

Our astronomical system came originally from the plains of Chaldea. The Babylonians divided the face of the heavens into constellations of stars, and named these after their supposed influence, or from their resemblance to various fantastic forms.

Mathematics, measures of time and capacity, weights and scales, laws and government, and everything known in ancient times, received study and attention, while the arts of building, sculpture, painting, gem-engraving, metal-work, weaving, and many others made proportionate progress.

In spite of the skill and knowledge of the Babylonians, and their wonderful progress in arts and sciences, they had a religion of the lowest and most degrading kind. True insight into natural phenomena was prevented, and progress beyond the surface of things stopped by a religion which had a multitude of gods, who were supposed to bring about in an irregular and capricious manner all the changes in nature and all the misfortunes which happened to the people; thus foresight and medicine were neglected, and unavailing prayers and useless sacrifices offered to propitiate the deities who were imagined to hold the destiny of the human race in their hands.

In the hands of some of the nobler poets of the Babylonians their mythology received a polish and finish, and was woven together into such graceful mythical forms, that their works may compare with those of Greece and Rome; but among the bulk of the people a low and sensual view was taken of all these matters, and their worship was nothing better than an adoration of stocks and stones.

The Babylonians were essentially a peaceful race. War was seldom indulged in by them, except it was forced upon them, either by their political position or through the action of states outside their own borders. Only once in their history are they known to have made a great empire, and that was in the time of Nebuchadnezzar.

The wonderful system of writing, called, from the shape of the characters, cuneiform, or wedge-shaped, was invented by the original Turanian inhabitants of Babylonia.

The characters were originally hieroglyphics, representing objects or combinations of objects, or symbolizing ideas. The pronunciation attached to the characters was accordingly the name of the object or idea which they signified in the ancient Babylonian language. In course of time the characters came to be used, not only to represent objects and ideas, but also to denote mere sounds. Thus the character which signified "a memorial," *mu* in the ancient language, came also to express simply the pronunciation of the first personal pronoun *mu*. When the characters were subsequently borrowed by Semitic tribes akin to the Hebrews and Arabs, and the ancestors of the later Babylonians and Assyrians, the sounds attached to the characters, which had been significant in the older language, became so many mere phonetic values; *mi*, for instance, signified "black" in the older, so-called Accadian, language, but it was simply a meaningless phonetic value in the later Assyrian.

The chief cities of Babylonia were the following:—

	Now represented by
Ur or Uru, literally "the City" ...	Mugheir.
Erech or Uruk	Warka.
Nipur, the city of Bel	Niffer.
Larsa, perhaps the Ellasar of Genesis xiv.	Senkereh.

	Now represented by
Babylon or Babel, originally called Ca-dimirra, "Gate of God" ...	Hillah.
Agadé (Accad), near Sippara ...	Part of Abu-Habba.
Tiggaba or Kute (Cuthah)	Tel Ibrahim.
Kisu or Kis	Hymar.
Sippara or Sepharvaim, the city of the sun-god	Abu-Habba.
Zirgulla	Zerghul.
Dur or Diru, literally "The Fortress"	Déyr.
Eridu, in the south-east of Babylonia	Abu-Shahrein.
Duran or Duban	Site unknown.
Karrak or Nisin	Site unknown.
Amarda or Marad	Site unknown.
Abnunna or Mullias or Umliyas ...	Site unknown.

Accadian literature was very extensive, and the libraries with which the country was stocked were full of treatises on all the branches of knowledge pursued by the ancient Chaldeans. One of the most famous of these libraries was that at Agadé, established by Sargon. It contained the great Babylonian work on astronomy and astrology in seventy books, which was called the "Illumination of Bel," and was afterwards translated into Greek by the historian Berosus.

Part of the catalogue of the library has come down to us, having been preserved in a copy made for the library of Assur-bani-pal, at Nineveh, and it includes treatises on the conjunction of the sun and the moon, on the movements of Mars and Venus, and on comets, which are termed "stars with a tail behind and a corona in front," as well as a direction to the student, who is told to write down the number of the tablet or book he wants to consult, and the librarian will thereupon hand it to him. It must be remembered that most of the literature of the Babylonians was stamped upon the clay so abundant in the country, the clay being afterwards hardened in the fire, a comparatively small portion of it being written upon papyrus, and hence a clay tablet became synonymous with a book. Another famous library was at Senkereh, or Larśa, which was rich in mathematical works. Some of these, one a table of squares and another of cubes, are now in the British Museum. Under Nebuchadnezzar Babylon enjoyed two libraries, and there seems to have been a very old one at Ur. The legends relating to the Deluge were brought to Nineveh from the library of Erech, and one of the legends of the Creation from the library of Cuthah. Attached to the library was an observatory, and the astronomer-royal, as we may term him, had to send fortnightly reports of his observations to the king. Some of these we possess, and translations of them will be found in the "Records of the Past," Vol. I., 155–159.

A very curious portion of the Accadian literature is a collection of charms and formulæ of exorcism, which seems to belong to the very earliest period of Babylonian history. There are magic formulæ of all kinds, some to ward off sorcery, some to bewitch other persons. Closely connected with these are various treatises on divination and lists of omens by which it was believed the future might be known. Thus there are tables of omens from dreams, from births, from the inspection of the hand or the entrails of animals, and from the objects a traveller meets with on the road. The following translation will give some idea of these curious tables:—

"(If a blue dog enters a palace, that palace) will be burned.
(If) a yellow dog enters a palace, exit from that palace will be baneful.
(If) a spotted dog enters a palace, that palace will give its peace to the enemy.
(If) a dog goes to a palace and kills some one, that palace is deprived of peace.

(If) a dog goes to a palace and lies down on a bed, that palace none with his hand will take.
(If) a dog goes to a palace and lies down on the throne, that palace will be burned."

Some of the omens are hardly likely to happen, however desirable their consequences may be. Thus we are told that "when a sheep bears a lion, the arms of the king will be powerful, and the king will have no rival." Others of them are obvious enough in their connection; "to dream of bright fire," for instance, "forebodes a fire in the city," and "the sight of a decaying house" was a sign of misfortune to its occupant. Here is a specimen of the exorcisms adopted to drive away evil spirits and the diseases they were imagined to occasion:—

"The noxious god, the noxious spirit of the neck, the spirit of the desert, the spirit of the mountains, the spirit of the sea, the spirit of the morass, the noxious cherub of the city, this noxious wind which seizes the body (and) the health of the body: O, spirit of heaven, remember! O, spirit of earth, remember!

"The burning spirit of the neck which seizes the man, the burning spirit which seizes the man, the spirit which works evil, the creation of the evil spirit:

O, spirit of heaven, remember! O, spirit of earth, remember!

"Wasting, want of health, the evil spirit of the ulcer, spreading quinsey of the gullet, the violent ulcer, the noxious ulcer: O, spirit of heaven, remember! O, spirit of earth, remember!

"Sickness of the entrails, sickness of the heart, the palpitation of a sick heart, sickness of bile, sickness of the head, noxious colic, the *agitation* of terror, flatulency of the entrails, noxious illness, lingering sickness, nightmare: O, spirit of heaven, remember! O, spirit of earth, remember!"

The most dreaded of the powers of evil were the seven "baleful" spirits or winds, originally the storm-clouds, of whom it was said by an ancient poet of Eridhu: "Those seven in the mountain of the sunset were begotten: those seven in the mountain of the sunrise did grow up. In the deep places of the earth have they their dwelling: in the high places of the earth have they their name." One of the formulæ of exorcism contains the following hymn in reference to them:—

"Seven (are) they, seven (are) they.
In the abyss of the deep seven (are) they.
In the brightness of heaven seven (are) they.

In the abyss of the deep in a palace (was) their growth.
Male they (are) not, female they (are) not.[1]
Moreover the deep (is) their pathway.
Wife they have not, child is not born to them.
Law (and) kindness know they not.
Prayer and supplication hear they not.
(Among) the thorns of the mountain (was) their growth.
To Hea (the god of the sea) (are) they hostile.
The throne-bearers[2] of the gods (are) they.
Disturbing the watercourse in the canal are they set.
Wicked (are) they, wicked (are) they.
Seven (are) they, seven (are) they, seven twice again (are) they."

The hymns to the seven wicked spirits introduce us to the great collection of hymns to the gods, which was compiled B.C. 2000, and formed at once the Chaldean Bible and liturgy. M. Lenormant has aptly compared it with the Rig-Veda of ancient India. Like the latter, it embodied hymns of various dates and authorship, and it seems to have been put

[1] The Accadian text, in accordance with the respect paid to women in Accad, reverses this order.

[2] This illustrates the verse in the account of the Deluge which describes how, in the course of the storm, "the throne-bearers went over mountain and plain."

together at the time of a great religious reform, when the Shamanistic beliefs of the early Accadians were fused into the organized polytheism of their Semitic conquerors. As an example of these hymns may be quoted one of those which are addressed to Samas, the sun-god :—

"O Lord, the illuminator of darkness, thou that openest the face (of sorrow),
Merciful God, the setter up of the fallen, the supporter of the sick,
Unto thy light look the great gods,
The spirits of earth all of them bow before thy face,
The language of praise like one word thou directest,
The host of their heads bow before the light of the mid-day sun.
Like a wife thou submittest thyself, joyfully and kindly :
Yea, thou art their light in the vault of the distant heaven,
Of the broad earth their banner art thou.
Men far and wide bow before thee and rejoice."

In another hymn, Merodach, a form of the sun-god and benefactor of mankind, is thus made to address the lightning, which is metaphorically called the scimitar, wherewith he smote the dragon Tihamtu in the war of the gods :—

"The sun of fifty faces, the lofty weapon of my divinity, I bear.

The hero that striketh the mountains, the propitious sun of the morning that is mine, I bear.

My mighty weapon, which like the sacrificial flame devours in a circle the corpses of the fighters, I bear.

The striker of mountains, my murderous weapon of Aṇu (the god of the sky), I bear.

The striker of mountains, the fish with seven tails, that is mine, I bear.

The terror of battle, the destroyer of rebel lands, that is mine, I bear.

The defender of conquests, the great sword, the falchion of my divinity, I bear.

That from whose hand the mountain escapes not, the hand of the hero of battle, I bear.

The delight of heroes, my spear of battle, (I bear).

My crown which strikes against men, the bow of the lightning, (I bear).

The crusher of the temples by rebel lands, my club and buckler of battle, (I bear).

The lightning of battle, my weapon of fifty heads, (I bear).

The *thunderbolt* of seven heads, like the huge serpent of seven heads, (I bear).

Like the serpent that beats the sea, (which attacks) the foe in the face.

The devastator of forceful battle, lord over heaven

and earth, the weapon of (seven) heads, (I bear).
That which maketh the light come forth like day, the god of the east, my burning power, (I bear).
The establisher of heaven and earth, the fire-god, who has not his rival, (I bear).
The weapon which (fills) the world (with) overwhelming fear,
In my right hand mightily made to go; (the weapon that) of gold (and) crystal
Is wrought for admiration, my God who ministers to life, (I bear)."

Still more remarkable is a penitential psalm, from which the following verses may be selected:—

"O my Lord, my transgression (is) great, many (are) my sins.
O my God, my transgression (is) great, my sins (are many),
O my Goddess, my transgression (is) great, my sins (are many).
O my God, that knowest (that) I knew not, my transgression (is) great, my sins (are many).
O my Goddess, that knowest (that) I knew not, my transgression (is) great, my sins (are many).
The transgression (that) I committed I knew not.
The sin (that) I sinned I knew not.
The forbidden thing did I eat.
The forbidden thing did I trample upon.

My Lord in the wrath of his heart has punished me.
God in the strength of his heart has overpowered me.
The Goddess upon me has laid affliction and in pain has set me.
God, who knew (that) I knew not, hath pierced me.
The Goddess, who knew (that) I knew not, hath caused darkness.
I lay on the ground and no man seized me by the hand.
I wept, and my palms none took.
I cried aloud; there was none that would hear me.
I am in darkness and trouble; I lifted not myself up.
To my God my (distress) I referred; my prayer I addressed.
The feet of my Goddess I embraced.
To (my) God, who knew (that) I knew not, (my prayer) I addressed.

* * * * * *

O my God, seven times seven (are) my transgressions, my transgressions (are) before me."

Of a very different character is the following prayer after a bad dream (W. A. I., iv., 66-2):

"May my God give rest to my prayer. . . .
May my Lord (grant) a merciful return (from trouble).
This day directs unto death the terrors (of night).
O my Goddess, be favourable unto me and hear my prayer.

May she deliver (me) from my sin; may my offering be accepted.
May the Deity deliver, may she be gracious to (my) gift.
My transgression may the seven winds carry away.
May the worm destroy (it), may the bird bear (it) aloft to heaven.
May the shoal of fish carry (it) away into the river.
May their tail and back receive (it) for me: may the waters of the river as they flow dissolve (it) for me.
Enlighten me also like an image of gold,
Like *rich* fat make me fat before thee.
Seize the worm, bury it alive: bury (it beneath) thy altar, thy multitudes seize.
With the worm cause (me) to pass and let me find protection with thee.
Dismiss me, and let a favourable dream come.
May the dream I dream be favourable; may the dream I dream be true.
The dream I dream to prosperity turn.
May Makhir, the god of dreams, rest upon my head.
Make me great, and to Bit-Saggal, the temple of the gods, the temple of Adar,
Unto Merodach, the merciful, for prosperity, to his prospering hands deliver me.
May thy descent be made known, may thy divinity be glorious,
May the men of my city celebrate thy mighty deeds."

All these hymns are translated from Accadian into Assyrian, the original Accadian text being placed in a parallel column on the left-hand side of the Assyrian translation.

The mythological poems given in Mr. Smith's "Chaldean Account of Genesis" are another proof of the extent to which poetry was cultivated in ancient Babylonia. Some of these are noticed subsequently, more especially the account of the Deluge and the great Izdhubar epic of which it forms an episode. This epic is a redaction of a number of independent poems of earlier date, the thread which runs through the whole and connects it together being the adventures of Izdhubar. The epic was probably put together in its present form about 2000 years B.C.; it is compiled on an astronomical principle, being divided into twelve books, each answering to a sign of the Zodiac and the Accadian month which was named after it. Thus the account of the Deluge is introduced into the eleventh book or lay, which corresponds with the sign Aquarius and the "rainy month" of the Accadian calendar.

The people of Accad were not neglectful of law. Probably the oldest table of laws in existence is the one which was copied and translated for the library of Nineveh, and in which we find that the life and status of the slave are recognized and provided for, and the mother is regarded as of more importance than the father, as is still the case with many Altaic tribes. The first two columns of the table are unfortunately too much broken to be read; the last two run as follows, beginning, it will be observed, with a list of legal precedents :—

"A certain man's brother-in-law hired (workmen) and built an enclosure on his foundation. From the house (the judge) expelled him.

In every case let a married man put his child in possession of property, provided that he does not make him inhabit it.

For the future (the judge may) allow a sanctuary to be erected in a private demesne.

(A man) has full possession of a sanctuary on his own high place.

The sanctuary (a man) has raised is confirmed to the son who inherits.

Effaced.

(A man) shall not (deny) his father and his mother.

(If a man) has named a town, but not laid the foundation-stone, he may change (the name).

This imperial rescript must be learnt.

Everything which a married woman encloses, she (shall) possess.

In all cases for the future (these rules shall hold good).

A decision. A son says to his father: Thou art not my father, (and) confirms it by (his) nail-mark (on the deed); (the son) gives him a pledge and pays him silver.

A decision. A son says to his mother: Thou art not my mother; his hair is cut off, (in) the city they exclude him from earth and water, and in the house imprison him.

A decision. A father says to his son: Thou art not my son; in house and brick building they imprison him.

A decision. A mother says to her son: Thou art not my son; in house and property they imprison her.

A decision. A woman is unfaithful to her husband, and says to him: Thou art not my husband; into the river they throw her.

A decision. A husband says to his wife: Thou art not my wife: half a maneh of silver he weighs out (in compensation).

A decision. A master kills (his) slaves, cuts them to pieces, injures their offspring, drives them from the land and makes them sick; his hand every day shall measure out a half-measure of corn (in requital)."

It is hardly necessary to describe Babylonian literature in further detail. It comprised beast-fables, riddles of a somewhat elementary kind, contract-tablets, deeds of sale, geographical lists, chronological tables, historical documents, copies of correspondence, and catalogues of the various animals, trees, stones, and other objects known to the Babylonians. Mathematics were not disregarded, and the figures of geometry were even made to serve the purposes of a superstitious divination. The insight thus afforded us into the literary activity and interests of a people whose very existence was almost forgotten but a few years ago, is one of the most remarkable revelations of the present century.

CYLINDRICAL SEALS.

CHAPTER II.

THE MYTHICAL PERIOD.

Origin and chronology of Babylonian history—The ten antediluvian kings of Berosus—The Flood—The Garden of Eden—The Izdhubar or Nimrod legends—Discoveries in Southern Babylonia.

In the antiquity of its civilization and history Babylonia has no rival in Asia, and the only country in the world which can compare with it, in these respects, is Egypt.

The history of Babylonia has an interest of a wider kind than that of Egypt, from its more intimate connection with the general history of the human race, and from the remarkable influence which its religion, its science, and its civilization have had on all subsequent human progress.

Its religious traditions, carried away by the Israelites who came out from Ur of the Chaldees,[1] have

[1] Gen. xi. 31.

through this wonderful people, become the heritage of all mankind, while its science and civilization, through the medium of the Greeks and Romans, have become the bases of modern research and advancement.

The extent of country comprehended under the name of Babylonia varied at different times, and it is impossible to fix the exact boundaries of the country at any period during the empire, for alternate conquest and defeat caused the boundaries to fluctuate continually. Generally speaking, it comprehended the country from near the Lower Zab to the Persian Gulf, about 400 miles long, and from Elam, east of the Tigris, to the Arabian Desert, west of the Euphrates, an average breadth of 150 miles.

Within this space, in early times, there were several kingdoms; and often, at a later period, local chiefs made themselves independent; for, the country, being peopled by several distinct tribes, there was a want of nationality and patriotism.

It is generally supposed that Babylonia was peopled in early times by Turanian tribes (tribes allied to the Turks and Tatars), and that these were conquered and dispossessed by the Semites. This change is very doubtful, although supported by much learned argument, grounded on the nature of the Babylonian language and writing.[1]

The history of Babylonia, from its own records, was translated into Greek by a Chaldean priest, named Berosus, who lived in the third century before the Christian era. The history of Berosus is lost, excepting an imperfect outline of his chronology and an account of the antediluvians, the Flood, and the time of Nebuchadnezzar and his successors.

The fragments of Berosus are so few, and it is so difficult to arrange his epochs, that they afford little aid in composing the history of the country.

On the other hand, the Babylonian and Assyrian

[1] I have left the contradiction between this passage and that on p. 16, because it expresses Mr. Smith's hesitation on the matter. Whether or not the early inhabitants and civilizers of Chaldea were allied to the Turks and Tatars of the present day —a point which is extremely doubtful—at all events they spoke an agglutinative language; that is, a language in which the relations of grammar are denoted, not by inflections, but by the attachment of independent or semi-independent words. The Accadian language, as it is usually termed, was closely allied to the dialects spoken in Elam, as well as to that of the Protomedic subjects of the Persian kings. M. Lenormant has argued ably in behalf of the view that this whole group of languages, though standing by itself, yet ultimately goes back to the same source as the Finnic family of tongues.—S.

inscriptions which supply most of our historical information, give very little insight into the chronology; so, even with the aids from ancient authors, the earlier part of the history is merely fragmentary. The Babylonian histories commenced with a description of the creation, similar in some respects to the one in Genesis, and then went on to relate that the Babylonians were first ruled by a king named Alorus, in whose time there came up out of the Persian Gulf a being named Oannes, who was half man, half fish, something like the Dagon of the Philistines. Oannes is said to have taught the Babylonians all their learning, and to have imparted to them the arts of civilized life.

According to the Babylonians, there were ten kings, beginning with Alorus, before the Flood; these ten agreeing in number with the ten patriarchs in Genesis; but an extravagant length was given by the Babylonians to this period, their statement being that the ten kings reigned for 432,000 years.

Beside the creature Oannes, they related that several similar beings came out of the Persian Gulf; and they otherwise adorned their narrative with marvels and legends to make up for the total want of real history.

The ninth of the kings before the Flood, according to the Babylonians, was named Ubara-tutu, and he corresponds in position to the Lamech of the Bible, who was father of Noah.

Ubara-tutu was succeeded by his son Adrahasis, or Hasisadra, who corresponds to the Noah of the Bible. In his time it is recorded that the whole of mankind had become wicked, and the Babylonian deities resolved to destroy the earth by a deluge. Hasisadra being a pious man, was commanded to build an ark, wherein himself, his family, and friends, and pairs of all animals should be preserved during the Flood. The Chaldean monarch accordingly built this vessel, and in it was saved.

The Chaldean story of the Deluge is so remarkable that I repeat it here as it is given on the tablets, namely as a speech put into the mouth of Hasisadra, or Noah. I append a series of notes of the parallel passages in Genesis for comparison.

Extract from the Eleventh Tablet of the Izdhubar Legends, giving the Chaldean account of the Deluge.

COLUMN I.

Line

8. Sisuthros speaks to him, even to Gisdhubar:
9. "Let me reveal to thee, Gisdhubar, the story of my preservation,
10. and the oracle of the gods let me tell to thee.
11. The city of Surippak, the city which, as thou knowest, is built on the Euphrates,
12. this city was already ancient when the gods within it
13. set their hearts to bring on a deluge, even the great gods,
14. as many as there are—their father Anu,
15. their king the warrior Bel,
16. their throne-bearer Adar,
17. their prince the lord of Hades.
18. Ea, the lord of wisdom, sat among them, and repeated their decree for the round boat: 'Round, round is the hull, the hull!
19. hear of the round boat and understand the hull,
20. O man of Surippak, son of Ubara-Tutu:
21. dig up the house, build the ship; save what thou canst of the germ of life.

Line

22. (The gods) will destroy the seed of life, but do thou live,
23. and bid the seed of life of every kind mount into the midst of the ship.
24. The ship which thou shalt build
25. 600 (?) cubits shall be the measure of its length (and)
26. 600 (?) cubits the measure of its breadth and its height.
27. (Above) the deep cover it in.'
28. I understood and spake to Ea my lord:
29. 'The building of the ship which thou hast commanded thus,
30. (if) it be done by me,
31. the children of the people and the old men (alike will deride me).'
32. Ea opened his mouth and said, he speaks to me his servant:
33. '(If they deride thee) thou shalt say unto them,
34. (Every one) who has turned against me and
35. (disbelieves the oracle that) has been given me,
36. . . . .
37. . . . . like the vaults (of the wide heaven)
38. . . . . . . I will judge above and below.
39. (But as for thee), shut (not) the door

(until) the time comes of which I will send thee word.
(Then) enter and turn the door of the ship, (and)
bring into the midst of it thy corn, thy property,
and thy goods,
thy (family), thy household, thy concubines, and
the sons of the people.
The (cattle) of the field, the wild beasts of the
field, as many as I would preserve,
I will send unto thee, and they shall keep thy door.'
Sisuthros opened his mouth and speaks;
he says to Ea his lord:
'(O my lord), no one yet has built a ship (in this
fashion)
on land to contain the beasts (of the field).
(The plan?) let me see, and the ship (I will build).
On the land the ship (I will build)
. . . . as thou hast commanded (me).'

COLUMN II.

On the fifth day (after it was begun)
in its circuit (?) 14 measures its hull (measured);
14 measures measured (the roof) above it.
I made it a dwelling-house (?) . . . I enclosed it.
I compacted it six times, I divided (its passages)
seven times,

Line

7. I divided its interior (seven) times.
8. Leaks for the waters in the midst of it I cut off.
9. I saw the rents and what was wanting I added.
10. Three *sari* of bitumen I poured over the outside.
11. Three *sari* of bitumen I poured over the inside.
12. Three *sari* of men, carrying baskets, who carried food on their heads,
13. I provided, even a *saros* of food for the people to eat,
14. while two *sari* of food the boatmen shared.
15. To (the gods) I caused oxen to be sacrificed;
16. I (established offerings) each day.
17. In (the ship) beer, food, and wine
18. (I collected) like the waters of a river, and
19. (I heaped them up) like the dust (?) of the earth, and
20. (in the ship) the food with my hand I placed.
21. (With the help) of Samas [the Sun-god] the compacting of the ship was finished;
22. (all parts of the ship) were made strong, and
23. I caused the tackling to be carried above and below
24. (Then) there went (into it) two-thirds (of my household):
25. all that I had heaped together; all that of silver I had heaped together;
26. all that of gold I had heaped together;

Line

27. all that I had of the seed of life I heaped together. The whole
28. I brought up into the ship, all my slaves and concubines,
29. the cattle of the field, the beasts of the field, the sons of the people, all of them did I bring up.
30. The season Samas fixed, and
31. he spake, saying: 'In the night will I cause the heaven to rain destruction.
32. Enter into the midst of the ship and shut thy door.'
33. The season came round (of which)
34. he spake saying: 'In the night will I cause the heaven to rain destruction.'
35. Of that day I reached the evening,
36. the day which I watched for with fear.
37. I entered into the midst of the ship and shut the door,
38. that I might close the ship. To Buzur-sadi-rabi the boatman
39. I gave the palace (the ark) with all its goods.
40. Then Mu-seri-ina-namari (the Water of Dawn at Daylight)
41. arose from the horizon of heaven (like) a black cloud.
42. Rimmon in the midst of it thundered, and
43. Nebo and the Wind-god go in front:

Line

44. the throne-bearers [the seven wicked spirits or storm-gods] go over mountain and plain:
45. Nergal the mighty removes the wicked:
46. Adar goes overthrowing all before him.
47. The spirits of earth carried the flood;
48. in their terribleness they sweep through the land;
49. the deluge of Rimmon reaches unto heaven;
50. all that was light to (darkness) was turned.

COLUMN III.

1. (The surface) of the land like (fire?) they wasted;
2. (they destroyed) all life from the face of the land;
3. to battle against men they brought (the waters).
4. Brother saw not his brother; men knew not one another. In heaven
5. the gods feared the flood, and
6. sought a refuge; they ascended to the heaven of Anu [*i.e.*, the highest heaven].
7. The gods, like a dog in his kennel, crouched down in a heap.
8. Istar cries like a mother,
9. the great goddess utters her speech:
10. 'All to clay is turned, and
11. the evil I prophesied in the presence of the gods,
12. according as I prophesied evil in the presence of the gods,

Line

13. for the destruction of my people I prophesied (it) against them ;
14. and tho' I their mother have begotten my people,
15. like the spawn of the fishes they fill the sea.'
16. Then the gods were weeping with her because of the spirits of earth ;
17. the gods on a throne were seated in weeping ;
18. covered were their lips because of the coming evil.
19. Six days and nights
20. the wind, the flood, and the storm go on overwhelming.
21. The seventh day, when it approached, the storm subsided, the flood
22. which had fought against men like an armed host
23. was quieted. The sea began to dry, and the wind and the flood ended.
24. I watched the sea making a noise,
25. and the whole of mankind was turned to clay ;
26. like reeds the corpses floated.
27. I opened the window, and the light smote upon my face ;
28. I stooped and sat down ; I weep ;
29. over my face flow my tears.
30. I watch the regions at the edge of the sea ;
31. a district rose twelve measures high.

Line

32. To the land of Nizir steered the ship;
33. the mountain of Nizir stopped the ship, and it was not able to pass over it.
34. The first day, the second day, the mountain of Nizir stopped the ship.
35. The third day, the fourth day, the mountain of Nizir stopped the ship.
36. The fifth day, the sixth day, the mountain of Nizir stopped the ship.
37. The seventh day when it approached
38. I sent forth a dove, and it left. The dove went and returned, and
39. found no resting-place, and it came back.
40. Then I sent forth a swallow, and it left. The swallow went and returned, and
41. found no resting-place, and it came back.
42. I sent forth a raven, and it left.
43. The raven went and saw the carrion on the water, and
44. it ate, it swam, it wandered away; it did not return.
45. I sent (the animals) forth to the four winds; I sacrificed a sacrifice.
46. I built an altar on the peak of the mountain.
47. I set vessels [each containing the third of an ephah] by sevens;

Line

48. underneath them I spread reeds, pine-wood, and spices
49. The gods smelt the savour; the gods smelt the good savour;
50. the gods gathered like flies over the sacrifices.
51. Thereupon the great goddess at her approach
52. lighted up the rainbow which Anu had created according to (his) glory.
53. The crystal brilliance of those gods before me may I not forget.

Column IV.

1. Those days I have thought of, and never may I forget them.
2. May the gods come to my altar [I said],
3. but may Bel not come to my altar,
4. since he did not consider but caused the flood,
5. and my people he consigned to the deep.
6. When at that time Bel at his approach
7. saw the ship, Bel stopped; he was filled with anger against the gods and the spirits of heaven:
8. 'Let none come forth alive! let no man live in the deep!'
9. Adar opened his mouth and spake, he says to the warrior Bel:

Line

10. 'Who except Ea can form a design?
11. Yea, Ea knows, and all things he communicates.'
12. Ea opened his mouth and spake, he says to the warrior Bel:
13. 'Thou, O warrior-prince of the gods,
14. why, why didst thou not consider but causedst a flood?
15. Let the doer of sin bear his sin, let the doer of wickedness bear his wickedness.
16. May the just prince not be cut off, may the faithful not be (destroyed).
17. Instead of causing a flood, let lions increase that men may be minished;
18. instead of causing a flood, let hyænas increase that men may be minished;
19. instead of causing a flood, let a famine happen that men may be (wasted);
20. instead of causing a flood, let plague increase that men may be (minished).
21. I did not reveal the determination of the great gods.
22. To Sisuthros alone a dream I sent, and he heard the determination of the gods.'
23. When Bel had again taken counsel with himself, he went up into the midst of the ship.
24. He took my hand, and bade me ascend,

Line

25. even me he bade ascend; he united my wife to my side.
26. He turned himself to us, and joined himself to us in covenant; he blesses us (thus):
27. 'Hitherto Sisuthros has been a mortal man,
28. but now Sisuthros and his wife are united together in being raised to be like the gods;
29. Yea, Sisuthros shall dwell afar off at the mouth of the rivers.'
30. They took me, and afar off at the mouth of the rivers they made me dwell."

This extract from one of the cuneiform tablets will serve to show the light which these documents throw on the Bible. The Chaldean legend of the Flood was in existence at least 2,000 years before the Christian era, and the scenes of the series of legends to which it belongs are carved on some of the most ancient Babylonian seals.

The Bible says nothing about the native country of Noah. The Chaldean legend, line 2, relates that he belonged to Surippak, a port near the entrance of the Euphrates into the Persian Gulf. The Chaldean legend agrees with Genesis vi. in ascribing the Deluge to the anger of the Deity at the wickedness of the world; and the name Hasisadra, given to Noah in the Chaldean story, expresses the character of the patriarch "reverent and attentive."[1]

The command to build the ark, in lines 21 to 44, may be compared with Genesis vi. 14–21. Unfortunately the size of the ark according to the Chaldean story is lost, so that we cannot compare the numbers with the statement of Genesis. The order to take the animals into the ark in line 43 parallels Genesis vi. 19, 20, and vii. 2, 3. The pouring bitumen over the inside and outside of the vessel (col. ii. lines 10, 11), is the same as Gen. vi. 14. The utter destruction of the world is given in col. ii. line 42 to col. iii. line 26, and Gen. vii. 17–23. With respect to the duration of the Deluge, there is a remarkable difference between the Bible and the Chaldean story. Here we may compare col. iii. lines 21, 34–38, and Gen. vii. 11, 17, 24, and viii. 3–6, 10, 12–14. The sending out of the raven is in col. iii. lines 42–44, and Gen. viii. 7; the dove in lines 38, 39, and Gen. viii. 8–12; but there is added in the Chaldean account the sending out of a swallow (lines 40, 41). In the Bible (Gen. viii. 4), the ark is said to have rested

[1] This is doubtful.—S.

on the mountains of Ararat. This, however, I believe does not mean the mountain now called Ararat, but a mountainous country south of this, and near the present Lake Van. From this region several mountain-chains run down towards the Persian Gulf, on the east of the Tigris. In this region, to the east of Assyria, was the land of Nizir, where the ark rested, according to the Chaldean account (col. iii. lines 32–36). There must be, however, at present, considerable difference of opinion as to the exact locality of the descent from the ark, as the limits of these geographical names are not defined.

The sacrifice of Noah (Gen. viii. 20), and the pleasure and blessing of God, reappear in col. iii. lines 46–50; and the resolution of the Lord not to destroy the world again by a flood compares with the statement in the inscription (col. iv. lines 17–20). The covenant and blessing of Noah (Gen. ix. 1–17) is given in col. iv. lines 26–29; but this includes a singular difference from the Biblical text. In the book of Genesis (v. 24) it is related that Enoch was translated. This remarkable passage is illustrated by col. iv. lines 28–30, and other places; but the Chaldean legend makes it Hasisadra or Noah who is translated for his piety, and not Enoch.

The whole of the Chaldean account of the Deluge is worthy of minute comparison with that in the book of Genesis, and will be found interesting, both in the points where it agrees with and those where it differs from the Biblical record. Until a few years back there was no confirmation of the book of Genesis earlier than the time of Alexander the Great; now, however, a flood of light is thrown on it by the cuneiform inscriptions, and it is highly probable that much more of the earlier part of Genesis will be found in these Chaldean texts. Fragments have been found of the account of the creation and building of the tower of Babel, and I have reason to believe that these are only parts of a series of histories giving full accounts of these early periods.[1]

[1] A full account of these tablets is given in Mr. Smith's "Chaldean Account of Genesis." Two versions of the history of the creation have been discovered, one an older one, which seems to agree with that adopted by Berosus, and another which must belong to a much later period, probably the seventh century B.C. According to the first version, the earth was originally a desert, and was then inhabited by nondescript creatures—men with the bodies of birds and the faces of ravens—until it was fitted for the abode of the present races of living beings. The second version of the account of the creation agrees very closely with that recorded in the first chapter of Genesis. The

The history of no other country is so likely to throw light on the earlier parts of the Bible as Babylonia, for here it is stated that the garden of Eden was situated, the first home of the human race (Gen. ii. 8, 17). Four rivers are given in this passage; two, the Euphrates and Tigris, are well known; the other two are considered, with great probability, to be two other streams of the same river system in Babylonia. Sir Henry Rawlinson has identified Eden with the region of Gan-duni, or Kar-dunias, in Babylonia, an

world is stated to have been made in six successive days, the sun, moon, and stars being formed on the fourth day, and the animals probably on the sixth. The account begins in this way:—

"At that time the heaven above (was) unnamed,
In the earth beneath a name (was) unrecorded:
The deep, too (was), was their first creator.
The great lady Tihamtu (the Deep) (was) the begetter of them all.
Their waters in one place were embosomed, and the fruitful herb (was) uncollected, the marsh plant (was) ungrown.
At that time the gods (the stars) were not made to go; none of them by name (were) recorded; order (was) not among them.
Then were made the (great) gods; (and these) Lakhmu and Lakhamu caused to go; until they were grown (they nurtured them).
The gods Assur and Kissar were made (by their hands).

identification which, although not proved, has many probabilities in its favour. In the inscriptions of Tiglath-Pileser II. it is stated that the land of Gan-dunias was watered by four rivers—the Euphrates, the Tigris, the Ukni, and the Surappi.

A length of days, a long (time passed, and) the gods Anu (Bel, and Hea were created), the gods Assur and Kissar (begat them)."

Connected with these creation tablets are others which describe the fall of man brought about by the tempter, the great dragon Tiamat (Tihamtu), or the "Deep," as well as another series, which recounts the war of Merodach, the sun-god, with Tiamatu and her allies. This war reminds us of the Biblical passage (Rev. xii. 7) in which it is said that "there was war in heaven: Michael and his angels fought against the dragon; and the dragon fought and his angels, and prevailed not." The fragments relating to the Tower of Babel are unfortunately very scanty. They confirm the statements of Greek writers, according to which the Babylonians related that the gods destroyed the Tower by winds. The name Bab-el signifies "Gate of God," and is a Semitic translation of the older Accadian name of the place, Ca-dimirra, which may possibly refer to the building of the Tower. As the Accadian name of the month Tizri (September) was "the month of the holy mound," while the deity who was connected with the building of the Tower was termed "the king of the holy mound," it is probable that the event in question was supposed to have taken place at the autumnal equinox. —S.

The Babylonians asserted that they had records written before the Flood, and that the cities of Babel, or Babylon, Sippara, Larancha, and Surippak were great cities before the Deluge.[1] Certainly, if there was a civilized race here for 1,000 to 1,500 years before the Flood, we might expect one day to find some traces of it; but as yet no contemporary monuments have been discovered which can be placed earlier than B.C. 3800, and even this date may be too early for our oldest known monuments.

The Babylonian traditions relate that after the Flood the people who were saved returned to Babylonia and repeopled the country; and Greek translations have preserved a few names of monarchs supposed to belong to the subsequent epoch; but nothing whatever is known of the state of the country or nature of the government.

The cuneiform inscriptions throw a little light on this obscure interval, but some of the accounts are overloaded with miraculous and impossible stories,

[1] Larancha must be identified with Surippak (or Suripkhu, as the name may also be read), since Xisuthrus is made a native of Larancha by Berosus, while he is called a native of Surippak in the cuneiform Deluge Tablets.—S.

from which it is difficult to separate the historical matter.

From these it appears that in early times this part of the world was divided into many small principalities, when there arose a hero whom I provisionally call Izdhubar, but who corresponds in my opinion to the Nimrod of the Bible. The Biblical account of Nimrod will be found in Gen. x. 8–12, and this really forms the only certain and authentic notice of the hero. There is, however, a mass of later tradition with respect to him which may be partly founded on the statements of Babylonian history; some of it, however, is evidently false.

Izdhubar, whom I identify with Nimrod, is reported to have been a local Babylonian chief, celebrated for his prowess; a mighty hunter and ruler of men, when some enemy, probably the chief of a neighbouring race, came down with a force of men and ships and attacked the city of Erech.

Erech was a large Chaldean city, near the Euphrates, about 120 miles south of Babylon. It is mentioned in Genesis as one of the capitals of Nimrod, and is now represented by the mounds of Warka. According to the Babylonian tradition, it was then devoted to the worship of Anu, god of heaven, and his wife, or consort, Anatu, and its ruler was a queen or goddess, named Ishtar, celebrated for her beauty and for her dissolute character.[1]

The enemy attacked the city and captured it, holding it in subjection for three years, when, by the will of the gods, it was delivered by Izdhubar, who then made it the chief city of his dominions. Izdhubar, after gaining Erech, was desirous to secure for his new court a celebrated sage, named Heabani, who appears to have been in the power of a monster. The monster was killed by order of Izdhubar, and Heabani came to Erech to the court of Izdhubar.

After the arrival of Heabani, he acted as astrologer and assistant to Izdhubar, and accompanied him in his various expeditions. Izdhubar then made war upon a chief named Humbaba, who ruled in a mountainous region clothed with pine-trees, and conquered him, annexing his dominions to Babylonia. Another chief, named Belesu, was then conquered, and probably many others whose names have been lost. According to the legend, the dominions of Izdhubar now reached from the Persian Gulf to the Armenian

[1] Ishtar was the Ashtoreth of the Bible, the Astarte of Greek writers.

mountains, and from the Euphrates to Elam, all the chiefs within this region being subject to him.

After this the story relates that Ishtar, queen of Erech, who appears sometimes as human, and sometimes as divine, conceived a passion for Izdhubar, and offered to marry him.

The character of Ishtar resembled that of the classical Venus. I think perhaps she may have been some notorious queen deified by the Babylonians; but it is quite possible that she was only a personification of human passion. According to the Babylonians, she had been first married to Dumuzi, Tammuz, or Adonis, whose tragical death was celebrated with great ceremony in the East (see Ezek. viii. 14). Afterwards, Ishtar is represented as leading a depraved life until she met Izdhubar and offered to marry him. Izdhubar refused her offer, and pointed out her faithless conduct, on which she became enraged, and mounting to heaven, complained to her father Anu, who was the ruling divinity of that region.

Anu being invoked by his daughter, at her request created a composite monster, a winged bull, which went to attack Izdhubar. The Babylonian monarch called his chiefs, and with the aid of Heabani they slew the animal. Ishtar then cursed Izdhubar, who had the animal cut up, and dedicated the horns in one of his temples.

Izdhubar now made a triumphal entry into Erech, and feasted his chiefs in the hall of his palace, at the same time making proclamation of his great deeds round the city. The tablets go on to describe various other exploits of Izdhubar and Heabani, but we are told that misfortune came and put an end to this prosperity. Heabani was killed by some poisonous animal, and Izdhubar himself was struck with disease. Up to this point, although the narrative is full of absurdities and miracles, it possibly had some foundation in fact; but the subsequent part of the history must be entirely mythical.

This latter portion of the narrative relates that Izdubar bitterly mourned over the death of Heabani, and then set out from the city of Erech to seek Hasisadra, the hero of the Flood, who was supposed by the Babylonians to be living with the gods somewhere near the Persian Gulf. It is remarkable that the Babylonian traditions surrounded with interest the region to the south of the country, where their own great rivers, the Tigris and Euphrates, poured into the sea. Out of this sea they relate that there arose Oannes, the composite monster who, according to

Berosus, taught civilization to the Babylonians. The building of the ark was placed here; and this sea was considered part of the great chaotic deep out of which the world was formed; while in this neighbourhood was the celestial region where the gods and spirits dwelt.

The description of the journey of Izdhubar is purely a romance. He visits the region where the giants control the rising and setting sun; he passes through a district of darkness, and emerges into a paradise. He afterwards visited the sea-coast, came into contact with a man named Siduri, and a woman named Sabitu, and later with a woman named Mua, to whom he relates the history of his connection with Heabani. About this time he falls in with a boatman named Urhamsi,[1] and they get out a boat and go to seek Hasisadra.

The purpose of Izdhubar is to ask the sage to cure him of his illness, and to attain himself, if he can, to the same immortality as that enjoyed by Hasisadra.

On the invitation of Izdhubar, Hasisadra is supposed to relate to him the story of the Flood (already given above); and then he instructs Urhamsi how to cure

[1] The reading of this name is really Nis-Ea.—S.

Izdhubar of his illness. Izdhubar after this returns to Erech, where he once more mourns over the lost Heabani.

Such is the outline of the story of Izdhubar from the cuneiform inscriptions. How much historical matter, if any, underlies the story, I cannot tell; but certainly no monuments of his age are known, and no confidence can be put in any of the details in their present form. The book of Genesis relates that after the Flood the people "journeyed from the east" to Shinar in Babylonia; and this statement of the Bible shows that the writer of Genesis pointed to the same region as the inscriptions for the descent from the ark. Nizir lies to the east of the Euphrates valley, and in journeying from it to Shinar a western course would be taken. On the other hand, the mountain now called Ararat lies quite to the north of the Euphrates valley.

Arrived in Babylonia from Nizir, the Bible describes the people as building the city of Babylon, and commencing there the erection of a tower, which work was stopped by Divine intervention. After the return to Babylonia, there arose a Cushite named Nimrod, who commenced an empire in the districts of Babel (Babylon), Erech (modern Warka, south of Babylon),

Akkad (near Sippara, north of Babylon),[1] and Calneh, which the Talmud identifies with Nipur or Niffer, east of Babylon, but which more probably lay near the Tigris. These four cities appear to have formed the centres or capitals of four states or districts into which in old times Babylonia was divided.

I have already suggested the identity of Nimrod with the Izdhubar of the inscriptions. Although this is not proved, it is probable; and there is certainly no other hero in the range of the Babylonian inscriptions likely to correspond with Nimrod.

The early Christian writers identified Nimrod with a king in the list of Berosus called Evechous, who is said to have reigned over Babylonia after the return of the inhabitants for 2,400 years, and they give after him the name of a second king Chomosbolus for 2,700 years. According to the history of Berosus, there reigned after the Deluge, commencing with Evechous, eighty-six kings, for a period of 34,080 or 33,091 years, down to the time when the Medes conquered Babylon. The long average of the reigns in this period proves

[1] Accad was rather a district distinct from Shinar (called Sumer in the inscriptions), but was so called from the city of Agadé, a part of Sippara, which the Semites pronounced Accad.

that we are not dealing here with history, but with mythical personages, or at best with traditionary heroes, whose reigns are greatly exaggerated.

It is curious that the narrative of Berosus, after this period of 34,080 years, commences the historical part of the work, not with a native dynasty, but with a foreign conquest, the first dynasty being stated to be Median,[1] and to have consisted of eight kings, who reigned for 224 years. Beside the name of Izdhubar, the cuneiform inscriptions supply two or three other names of kings belonging to the long mythical or traditionary period after the Flood; among these are Etanna, who built a city which may have been the same as Babel, Tammuz, and Ner. No monuments or remains of this period are known, but it is probable that there existed at one time in Babylonia rude and early monuments which were ascribed to this period; for we are told in the Izdhubar legends that that hero raised stone monuments in memory of his celebrated journey to Hasisadra.

[1] As the Median dynasty of Berosus seems to have derived its name, not from the Media of classical geography but from the Accadian word *mada*, "country," it is possible that the dynasty may, after all, have been a native one belonging to the "country" of Babylonia.—S.

The plain or "field" of Babylonia was called Edinna in the old Accadian language, a word which was borrowed by the Semitic conquerors of the country under the form of Edinu or Edin. This is clearly the Eden of the Old Testament, so that it is not surprising that the two main rivers of the garden of Eden are said to have been the Euphrates and the Hiddekhel. Hiddekhel is the Accadian name of the Tigris, *id Idikla* "or stream of Idikla." The garden planted in Eden may have been near the town of Eridu, now marked by the ruins of Abu-Shahrein, in the south of Babylonia, which in the second millennium before the Christian era stood on the sea-shore. At all events, Eridu is regarded as a sacred city in Babylonian literature; it is frequently termed "the good" or "holy," and near it was a forest or "garden" where grew "the holy pine-tree" identified with "the tree of life."

As Oannes, the mythical instructor of the Babylonians in the arts of civilised life, was supposed to have come from the waters of the Persian Gulf, we may infer that Chaldean culture was originally carried from the south to the north. One of its first seats may have been the city of Eridu. At any rate, it is in southern Babylonia that the earliest evidences of

E 2

Babylonian art and civilisation have been discovered. M. de Sarzec, French Consul at Bassorah, has recently excavated certain mounds in this part of the country known by the name of Tello. The inscriptions uncovered on the spot show that the city which once stood there was called Girsu or Sirgulla, and was governed by dynasties who belonged to the very dawn of Babylonian history. The monuments discovered by M. de Sarzec and now in the Museum of the Louvre fall into two classes. The first of these presents us with Babylonian art and the cuneiform system of writing in their very infancy. The art is rude; the cuneiform characters are still partially pictorial, and are written vertically rather than horizontally. These monuments are followed by others of a later period when art and culture have very considerably advanced. One of the rulers of Sirgulla during this later period was Gudea, son of Dungi, small bronze images of whom are in the British Museum as well as a mutilated statue of black marble. Several other statues have been sent to Paris by M. de Sarzec. They are seated, and on the top of one of the figures is a plan of the city, indicating perhaps that the statue is that of the royal architect. According to Dr. Oppert, some of the statues are of diorite, a stone which the inscriptions upon them state was brought from the land of Magan or the Sinaitic Peninsula. It is curious that one of the most remarkable products of Egyptian art is a diorite statue of King Khephren of the fourth dynasty, the builder of the second pyramid at Gizeh, and that the attitude and costume of this statue strikingly resemble those of the statues of Tello. It is therefore possible that an intercourse existed between Babylonia and Egypt at an early epoch, and that there was a school of sculptuary among the Egyptian colonists in the Peninsula of Sinai.

At the time when Sirgulla was at the height of its prosperity, the Semites had not as yet entered the country. The inscriptions found there are all composed in the Accadian dialect of Sumer. Northern Babylonia was apparently the first to be occupied by the Semitic settlers or invaders. If we are to trust an inscription of Nabonidos, this must have happened at a very remote period indeed. Nabonidos states that when he set about restoring the temple of the Sun-god at Sippara he first searched for the record of its original builder Naram-Sin, the son of Sargon I., a famous Babylonian monarch of whom more will be said further on. He then proceeds to say: "The cylinder of Naram-Sin the son of Sargon, which for three thousand two hundred years no king going before me had seen, Samas, the great lord of Beth-Parra, the temple, the seat of the joy of his heart, revealed to me." This would make the date of Naram-Sin B.C. 3850, and since Sargon seems to have reigned after the Semitic Babylonians had been long settled in the country, we should have to place their entry into Chaldea at least as early as B.C. 4000. But we do not at present know what grounds Nabonidos had for fixing the date of Naram-Sin, and until we do so, it is permissible to question its accuracy.

A fragmentary list of Babylonian dynasties places Sargon among "the kings who reigned after the Deluge, but not in chronological order," the object of the list being a purely philological one, that, namely, of giving the signification of certain royal names. There was, however, another list of the dynasties, which had a chronological purpose, and from which Berosus probably derived his information. Two extracts from this in what seems to have been a boy's lesson-book enumerate "the eleven kings of the dynasty of Babylon" and "the ten kings of the dynasty of Sisku." Sisku, if that is the right reading—which is very doubtful—may have been a name of Erech. The dynasties are as follows :—

The kings of Babylon :—

1. Sumu-abi, for 15 years.
2. Sumu-la-ilu, 35 years.
3. Zabu, his son, 14 years.
4. Abil-Sin, his son, 18 years.
5. Sin-muballidh, his son, 30 years.
6. Khammuragas, his son, 55 years.
7. Samsu-ilu-na, his son, 35 years.
8. Ebisu, his son, 25 years.
9. Ammi-satana, his son, 25 years.
10. Ammi-saduga, his son, 21 years.
11. Kit-satana, his son, 31 years

The kings of Sisku (?):—

Anman was king of Sisku.

Then came :

1. Ki-dingir-nibi.
2. Damki-ili-su.
3. Iskipal.
4. Sussi.
5. Gulkhisar.
6. Kir-gal-dubba, his son.
7. Adub-kalama, his son.
8. Akur-ulana.
9. Melam-kurkura.
10. Ea-ga.

The kings of Sisku probably preceded those of Babylon, among whom Zabu was already known to us as the founder of the temple of Anunit at Sippara. Khammuragas is perhaps to be distinguished from the monarch of the same name whose history will be recorded further on, though it is curious that both princes should have been succeeded by a son called Samsu-iluna. The names of Khammuragas and the last three kings of the dynasty are not Babylonian, but are derived from the language of the Kassi or Kossæans who inhabited the mountains east of Babylonia; we may therefore infer that Sin-muballidh married a Kassite princess.

CHAPTER III

CHALDEA, OR SOUTH BABYLONIA.

Nipur and Ur—Urukh and his buildings—The religion and civilization of Ur—Dungi—The kings of Karrak—The rise of Larsa.

In early times Babylonia appears to have consisted of several states, which in time became consolidated into one. Of these states our monuments make us first acquainted with one in the south, the capital of which was Ur. At this time our indications suggest that the parent city of Ur was Nipur, now Niffer, a city lying south-west of Babylon, between the Euphrates and Tigris. On the site of Niffer there are now the ruins of a considerable city, divided into two parts by the dry bed of a river, probably in ancient times a branch of the Euphrates.

Nipur was devoted to the worship of Bel, the great deity of the Babylonians, who was one of the three supreme gods; and joined with his worship was that of his consort Belat, or Mylitta, and the god Ninip, lord of war and hunting, who was called his son.

Of the time when Nipur was the leading city in this part of Babylonia, we have discovered no monuments; but immediately after, we find, when the monarchy of Ur arose, it was claimed that the god of Ur, the moon, was "the eldest son of Bel, the god of Nipur," the claim carrying with it evidently the assertion that he inherited the rule of his father, and his city the position of his father's seat, Nipur.

Ur, the city which thus appears to have succeeded Nipur as capital, is represented by the mounds of Mugheir, about six miles from the Euphrates on its western bank, about lat. 31°. It was probably not far from the old mouth of the Euphrates, but the river, in company with the Tigris, brings down so large an amount of material to deposit at its mouth, that the land rapidly accumulates at the head of the Persian Gulf, and the present mouth of the Euphrates is far from the original outlet of the river. The ruins of Ur are enclosed by a wall, something in the shape of a pear, and measuring about two miles round. The space round the town is full of graves of all ages, showing the long period through which the city flourished. This city was probably the Ur of the Chaldees, mentioned in Genesis xi. 28 as the birthplace of Abraham.

According to the ordinary chronology of our Bible, it was in the twentieth century before the Christian era when Abraham left his Chaldean home to migrate into Syria; and it is curious that so far as we can judge from the inscriptions, it was about this time that the city of Ur rose into importance.

The city of Ur was devoted to the worship of the moon-god, called in early times Ur, and the place itself appears to have been named after that divinity "the city of Ur."[1] The rise of Ur caused the worship of the moon-god to become famous, and to extend over the whole of the country, the Babylonians ever after esteeming this divinity in preference to Shamas, the sun-god, and they always considered the moon to be masculine, while sometimes the sun was represented as the son of the moon, and at other times as a female divinity.

The earliest known ruler of the city of Ur was a monarch whose name is very uncertain; it has been

[1] This is hardly correct. The title of the moon-god alluded to in the text is really Hur-ci, "protector of the land," while the true meaning of Uru or Ur is "the city."—S.

read provisionally by Sir H. Rawlinson as Urukh, and compared with the Orchamus of Ovid and the Arioch of Genesis: these identifications are, however, very uncertain.[1] We have no knowledge of the age of Urukh, but he cannot well be placed later than the twentieth century B.C., while he may have been much earlier. The period of Urukh marks the age when our known contemporary monuments begin; there must have been in many places earlier buildings, works of art, and inscriptions; but excavations in Babylonia have been so limited, that none have yet been brought to light. It is evident that the age of Urukh cannot be the starting-point of Babylonian civilization, because the remains of this period show the country well advanced in arts and sciences.

The art of building was well known, and had reached a high state of excellence; the material in general consisted of brick, either burnt or dried in

[1] It is probable that the true reading of the name is Lig-Bagas. At all events an inscription has been found on a cylinder which calls the king Dungi the son of Lig-Bagas, and this king Dungi is probably identical with the monarch of that name to be mentioned presently. The first part of the name in question is certainly to be read *Lig*, "a lion;" the second part is the name of the primeval goddess, the mother of the gods, called Zicum, or Zigara, "heaven," by the Accadians.—S.

the sun; but carving in stone was known and practised, and inscribed stone tablets, and cylindrical stone seals of this age are in existence showing the advance of the people in these directions. Writing with the conventional cuneiform characters was well known and practised, most of the bricks and stone objects being inscribed with legends in these characters. These inscriptions show that the language of the people was Semitic, although they were using a syllabary and style of writing which many scholars have supposed to be derived from a much earlier race.[1]

The government of the country appears then to have been in the hands of kings, of whom there were probably three or four; and under them were "patesi," or viceroys, who ruled in the different districts.

The religion of Babylonia, which was often modified in subsequent ages, was already woven into a poetic system, in which the gods were conceived of as begetting each other, holding rank in reference to each other, engaging in particular offices, and favouring each a particular locality or city.

[1] This is not quite correct, as several of the inscriptions of this age, like the proper names they contain, are not in Semitic, but in the Accadian, or agglutinative language of ancient Chaldea.—S.

The three great gods were Anu, lord of the heavens; Bel, lord of the visible world; and Hea, lord of the sea and infernal regions. Anu was originally worshipped at the city of Erech, but in later times the goddess Ishtar took his place at this seat; Bel had his chief seat at Nipur, and Hea at the city of Eridu. Sin, or the moon-god of the new capital Ur, was called eldest son of Bel; Samas, the sun-god; Nergal, god of war; Ninip, a similar divinity; Vul,[1] god of the atmosphere, with many others, were in great repute; while among the female divinities Anatu, goddess of life and death, who was the female form and complement of Anu; Anunit, goddess of Akkad;[2] Nana goddess of Erech; Beltis, wife of Bel; and Davkina, consort of Hea, were the most celebrated.

From the engravings on the seals of this period it appears that long, flowing, embroidered dresses were used, and ornamental articles of furniture. Urukh, the earliest known king of Ur, probably began his reign only in the district round his capital, and afterwards extended his dominion over most of Babylonia. We are entirely ignorant of the conflicts and triumphs which led to the establishment of his empire, and can

[1] Rather Rimmon.—S. [2] Or Agadé.—S.

only trace his power by the cities he ruled over, and the splendid edifices he raised. His reign appears to have been long and prosperous, and he was a greater builder than any other king excepting Nebuchadnezzar. At the city of Ur he built the temple of the moon-god, and a ziggurat, or temple-tower, lying in the northern part of the town. This tower was built on a mound about twenty feet high. The building, so far as it has been explored, consists of two stages, with some traces of a third, or upper stage ; the lower stage is 198 feet long by 133 feet broad, and the middle stage 119 feet long by 75 feet broad. The form of the superstructure and height of the stages have not been made out, and it is quite likely that there were originally more stages. The body of the building consists of sun-dried bricks, with a facing ten feet thick, composed of burnt bricks, each side being further strengthened by shallow buttresses of the same material.

This temple-tower was building during the reign of Urukh, and was left unfinished at his death.

Numerous other buildings at the city of Ur were raised by Urukh, and among them a palace called the house of Rubu-tsiru, or "the supreme prince."

At the city of Larsa, Urukh built the temple of the

sun, called the house of "Parra," and at the city of Erech he built the temple of the heavens, which had originally been dedicated to the god Anu, but was now devoted to the worship of Ishtar, or Venus. At Nipur he built a temple to Bel, and a second to the goddess Belat or Beltis, the consort of Bel. At Zerghul he built a temple to Sar-ili, or the king of the gods. It is probable that further excavations would reveal numerous other buildings raised by this monarch, but our present information is in every way scanty.

Urukh was succeeded by his son Dungi, who ruled as far north as Babylon. Dungi finished the tower at Ur, rebuilt the temple of Erech, and built a temple at Babylon.

A fine cylindrical seal of the age of Urukh was discovered by Ker Porter, but subsequently lost; another, very similar, of the age of Dungi, is now in the British Museum.

Several successors of Dungi are known: these kings have in most cases their names compounded with the name of the moon-god, but the pronunciation of this element is uncertain; the inscriptions render it Ur,[1]

[1] Rather Hur-ci.—S.

Agu, Aku, Ida, and Sin. The worship of the moon became very celebrated on account of this deity being god of the capital city.

The city of Ur in time declined, and another capital arose, named Nisin, or Karrak : the position of this place is unknown, but it was probably not far from Nipur.

There is a difference in character between the inscriptions of the kings of Ur and those of Karrak, which suggests the idea that they belonged to two different races.

Among the kings of Karrak the two most important appear to have been Ismi-dagan and Libit-istar. Ismi-dagan repaired some of the buildings of Urukh. Some writers have placed him in the nineteenth century B.C., supposing him to be the same as an Ismi-dagan who then ruled in Assyria. Libit-istar has also left some remains. There is in the British Museum a fragment of a beautiful inscription relating his offerings in the temple of Bel, and a dream which the king afterwards had.

The city of Karrak, like Ur, declined, and the ruling power passed to the city of Larsa, on the east side of the Euphrates, now represented by the ruins of Senkereh. The kings of Larsa had, however, at

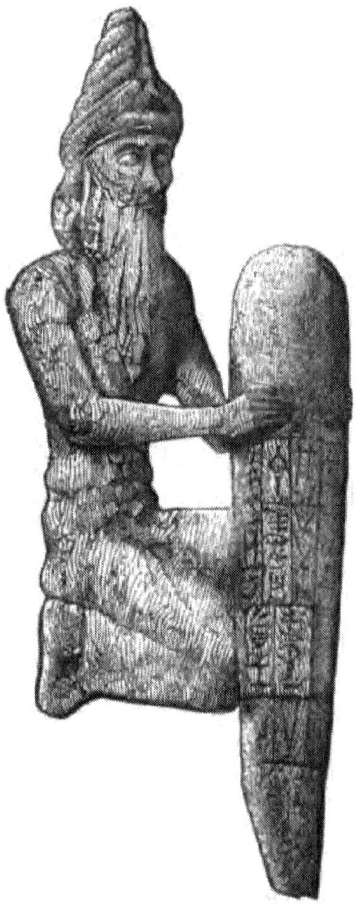

BRONZE IMAGE OF KING GUDEA.

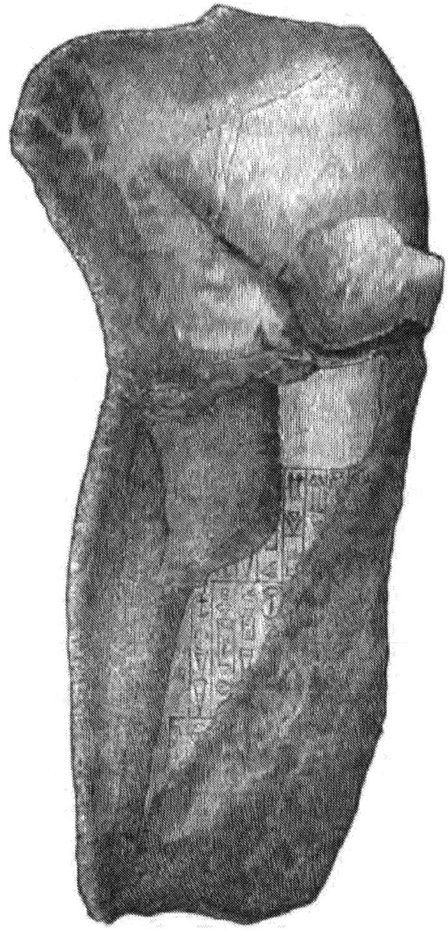

BLACK MARBLE TORSO OF KING GUDEA,
MUCH MUTILATED.

first a very limited kingdom, only embracing the region of Ur and Larsa; but it gradually grew in importance until it came under the influence of the rulers of Yamutbal, on the east of the Tigris. The first of these known was Simti-silhak: his son was named Kudur-mabuk. Kudur-mabuk gained such influence that he virtually ruled at Larsa, and placed his own son, Rim-agu, or Riagu, on the throne there. Kudur-mabuk and his son then made a joint attack on Karrak, and capturing the city, put an end to the power of that capital. Subsequent conquests completed their dominion, which extended over most of Babylonia. The Chaldeans considered the fall of Karrak so important that they commenced to count from it as an era, and used it for their computations until the fall of Larsa.

Riagu governed well under the regency of his father, and built temples, excavated canals, and engaged in various other valuable works. After about thirty years of peace, the dominions of Riagu were attacked by Hammurabi,[1] another of these kings, and the south of the country was conquered, never again to be the chief seat of power.

[1] Or Hammuragas.

CHAPTER IV.

UPPER BABYLONIA.

Cities of Upper Babylonia—Agu-kak-rimi—Sargon I.—Naram-Sin—Hammurabi—Babylon made the capital—The successors of Hammurabi, and the Kassite dynasty—Intercourse with Assyria—The Assyrian conquest of Babylonia.

THE region of Upper Babylonia, probably the Akkad of the inscriptions, included all the country north of the city of Nipur, or Niffer. This region was the classical land of cuneiform literature, and from its terra-cotta libraries came most of the great works which were copied in Assyria.

The following were the principal towns:—

Babylon, a city said to have been built in very early times, but which remained for some centuries of secondary importance. It became at length capital of the country, a position it held for more than 1,200 years, until the Greek conquest of Asia.

Borsippa, south-west of Babylon, a famous city, supposed to be the site of the Tower of Confusion.

Sippara, which consisted of two cities, one dedicated to Shamas, the other to Anunit.

THE TEMPLE OF NEBO AT BORSIPPA: BIRS NIMRŪD.

Akkad, near Sippara, the capital before the rise of Babylon; Kisu and Harriskalama, two twin cities near Babylon.

Cutha, a great city east of Babylon.

The early history of Upper Babylonia is unknown. All we can do respecting it is to notice some of the names of the monarchs and their works: their dates and succession have not been discovered; but it is probable that they were contemporary with the kings of Lower Babylonia.

One of these kings was Agu, or Agu-kak-rimi, who ruled at Babylon, and restored the temple of Bel at that site. It appears by his inscription that before his time Babylonia had been worsted in war, and the images of Merodach and his consort Zirat-banit, the great gods of Babylon, had been carried captive into the land of Hani, a region, the position of which is uncertain, but which probably lay somewhere north-east of Babylon. Agu sent an officer, and recovered the images; but his narrative leaves the impression that they were ransomed, and that Babylon had at this time only a subordinate position.

Zabu, another of these kings, is only known as the builder of the temples of Samas and Anunit at Sippara.

The most celebrated line of sovereigns in Upper Babylonia was the race of the kings of Akkad, and according to Nabonidos, they reigned about B.C. 3800 to 3650. The greatest of these sovereigns was named Sargon, which means "the right" or "true king." He emerged from a position of obscurity, being husbandman to a water-carrier, and he has left a curious inscription in which he claims relationship with the former royal family. He relates that his father's brother ruled over the country, and that his mother concealed his birth, and placing him in an ark of reeds daubed over with bitumen, abandoned him on the Euphrates. Akki, a water-carrier, going to the river, is said to have discovered the ark and brought up the child as his own.[1] We are ignorant of the circumstances which led to the accession of Sargon, but another of his inscriptions relates a number of the prominent events of his reign.

The Elamites, on the east of Babylonia, being troublesome, he made an expedition against them, and defeated them; then he attacked the Hittites, or Syrians, on the Upper Euphrates, and conquered these, claiming the rule of the four races or regions.

Within Babylonia itself were other states with which

[1] The inscription which relates this legend can hardly belong to the age of Sargon, but must be of much later date.—S.

Sargon now came in contact, and which he subdued, reducing the whole of the country to his sway.

After this, two expeditions against the Syrians followed, in both of which the Babylonian monarch claims the victory. Then he started on a long march of conquest to the Mediterranean. He appears to have met with considerable opposition, and the expedition lasted for three years. During it he reached the Mediterranean, and planting his standard by its shores, left there a tablet to commemorate the extent of his conquests. The next expedition of Sargon was against Kastu-bila of Kazalla, and after defeating him, he wasted the country.

Sargon had hitherto been successful, and had imposed his yoke on several of his neighbours. He had now to meet a formidable revolt. We are told that the elders of all the people revolted against him, and his people besieged him in his capital Akkad.[1] When his preparations were completed, Sargon sallied out of his city, and attacked and routed the revolters, putting an end to this disaffection. Once more assured at home, Sargon recommenced his foreign wars, and invading the neighbouring land of Subarti,[2]

[1] Or Agadé.

[2] Subarti was the highlands of Mesopotamia.

wasted it with fire and sword, bringing back much spoil to his capital.

Sargon was a great builder as well as a warrior. He rebuilt the city of Akkad,[1] raised a palace there, and either built or restored the great temple of Anunit; and he founded a city, which he called Dur-Sargina, on the site of an old Chaldean town. Sargon probably reigned forty-five years, during which time he had extended the power of the kingdom of Akkad [2] from Dilmun on the Persian Gulf to the shores of the Mediterranean; but on every side lay kingdoms only under tribute, which revolted as soon as the sceptre passed into less vigorous hands.

Sargon was succeeded by Naram-Sin, his son, who conquered the kingdom of Apirak; and later on, the land of Maganna, the "ship region." This name Maganna is also applied to Egypt in later times,[3] but it is more probable that the Maganna of Naram-Sin was a region on the Persian Gulf.

Naram-Sin completed Bit-ulbar, the temple of Anunit, which was left unfinished at his father's death.

[1] Or Agadé. [2] Or Agadé.

[3] Or rather to the peninsula of Sinai. It is very questionable whether Mr. Smith was right in interpreting the word as "ship's region."—S.

After the time of Naram-Sin, the history of the kingdom of Akkad[1] is obscure, and nothing is certain until we come to the reign of Hammurabi.

The reign of Hammurabi appears to mark an era in Babylonian history. Before his time we hear of kingdoms at Ur, Larsa, Akkad,[2] Babylon, Karrak, and other places; and occasionally we find powerful monarchs, like Urukh and Sargon, ruling all the country; but we have no evidence that the whole of Babylonia was permanently united into a single monarchy before the time of Hammurabi. The race to which Hammurabi belonged is unknown,[3] and complete obscurity hangs over his early history. In the absence of any certain information, it is assumed that he commenced the Arabian dynasty of Berosus, and that he reigned near the middle of the sixteenth century B.C. Hammurabi ruled at Babylon, while Rim-agu and his father, Kudur-mabuk, possessed the south and east of the country. Hammurabi made war against Kudur-mabuk and his son, defeated their forces and overran the whole of Babylonia, uniting the country as far as the Persian Gulf into one monarchy.

[1] Or Agadé. [2] Or Agadé.
[3] He was probably a Cassite from Elam.—S.

The influence and political power of the southern cities now departed, and henceforth Babylon stands forth as the sole capital of the country. Hammurabi took the titles of king of Babylon, king of Sumir and Akkad, and king of the four races, and fixed his court at the city of Babylon, where he increased the magnificence or the worship of Merodach, or Bel, the Belus of the Greeks; and this deity ever afterwards held the first position among the gods of the country.

Excepting a short statement of his conquest of Rim-agu and his father, and an incidental notice of his conquest of Surippak, nothing is known of the wars and triumphs of Hammurabi; but he has left several notices of his buildings, showing the resources of his kingdom, the extent of his dominion, and the activity of his rule.

At the city of Kisu, on the east of Babylon, now represented by the mounds of Hymer, Hammurabi restored the temple called Mite-urris,[1] dedicated to the god Zamama, and built a ziggurat or tower, the top of which is said to have reached to heaven. This monarch also restored the temple called Silim-kalama,

[1] Rather Mite-tassak, "the dwelling (?) of the hero."

and built a city on the Tigris, named Kara-samas. At the city of Zarilab, in Chaldea, he built a temple to the goddess of the place, and he rebuilt the temple of Samas at Larsa (now Senkereh), raising there another of those remarkable ziggurats.

Another great work of Hammurabi was a canal, called Hammurabi-nuḫus-nisi; he also built a palace at the city of Kilmad (now Kalwadha), near Baghdad, and here bronze rings, belonging to some of his mace-heads, have been discovered. During the reign of Hammurabi one of the annual floods, of greater volume than usual, destroyed the city of Abnuna, or Umliyas. Hammurabi probably reigned about ten years after he conquered the kingdom of Larsa. He was succeeded by Samsu-iluna, a monarch of whose reign little is known. Samsu-iluna excavated a famous canal, which was afterwards reckoned among the rivers of Babylonia. This canal he named Samsu-iluna-nagab-nuhsi. He also repaired the city of Dur-sargina, and made images overlaid with gold, which he dedicated in the temple of Saggal, at Babylon, to Merodach, and in the temple of Parra, at Larsa, to Samas. After the reign of Samsu-iluna complete darkness comes over Babylonian history: no records of the succeeding period have been found, and only a few obscure and doubtful names are known. Among these we may perhaps count the name of Saga-saltiyas, a monarch who is only known as the restorer of the temples of Sippara. There were two cities of Sippara, one devoted to the worship of Anunit, the other to the worship of Samas; the temples at these places were raised by an ancient king, named Zabu, and having fallen into decay were rebuilt by Saga-saltiyas.

During the reign of another of these monarchs, named Harbi-sipak, there were some controversies between Assyria and Babylonia. These disputes form the first intercourse between the two countries known directly from the inscriptions. Probably a little time after the reign of Harbi-sipak[1] connected history begins in Babylonia with the reign of Kara-indas, who lived about the middle of the fifteenth century B.C. Kara-indas takes the titles "king of Babylon, king of Sumir and Akkad, king of Kassu, and king of Karu-duniyas." From this time the title "king of Kar-duniyas" was the general title given to Babylonian sovereigns by the Assyrians in their records. During

[1] The name should probably be rather read Murgas-Sipak. —S.

the reign of Kara-indas, Assur-bel-nisi-su ruled over Assyria, and a treaty was made between the two powers respecting the boundary-line of these states. It is very likely that some provinces were in dispute, and that the limits of each territory varied according to the power of successive kings. The line of separation at this time is not known, but it was probably a little north of the 35th parallel of latitude, between the Lower Zab, which was considered an Assyrian river, on the one side, and the river Turnat (modern Adhem), which was considered to be Babylonian, on the other.

After Kara-indas Burna-buriyas reigned over Babylonia, about B.C. 1425. Burna-buriyas restored some Babylonian buildings. He continued the peace with Assyria, and confirmed the treaty which his predecessor had made respecting the boundaries of Babylonia. Shortly after this, about B.C. 1400, Assur-ubalid, king of Assyria, to cement the peace between Babylonia and his own country, gave his daughter Muballidat-Serua in marriage to the king of Babylon. It is not known who was then on the Babylonian throne, but shortly afterwards, about B.C. 1380, Kara-hardas,[1] the

[1] Rather to be read Kara-Murdas, "servant of the god Murudas,' or Bel.—S.'

fruit of this marriage, and, therefore, the grandson of the king of Assyria, began to reign in Babylonia. The tribe of Kassu now appear on the scene as the leading people in Babylonia. They were first mentioned in an inscription of Agu-kak-rimi, and again in the time of Kara-indas; they were perhaps related to the tribe of the same name living north of Elam; but nothing is known of their previous history or their advent in Babylonia. The Kassu being dissatisfied with the Assyrian influence at court, and disliking the foreign connections of the king, made a revolt against him, and slew him, setting up in his place a man named Nazi-bugas, whom the Assyrians assert to have had no right to the throne, and not to have been connected with the royal family.

It appears that this revolution was not effected without opposition, and there was a party favourable to the restoration of the old line. Bel-nirari, king of Assyria B.C. 1375, who was son of Assur-ubalid, and therefore uncle of the murdered king of Babylon, resolved to avenge his death; and marching into Babylonia routed the Kassu and slew Nazi-bugas, placing the crown on the head of a son of Burna-buriyas, supposed to be Kur-galzu, or Kuri-galzu. This interference of Assyria in the affairs of Babylonia was the commencement of an unfortunate policy, and inaugurated a series of wars between the two countries which lasted two hundred years.

Kuri-galzu, although he attained his throne through Assyrian aid, does not appear to have trusted his allies, and he built a strong city, called Dur-kuri-galzu (now Akkerkuf), near Baghdad, to form a defence in the northern part of his dominion. He also restored some of the Chaldean temples, and was considered one of the most successful Babylonian monarchs.

Kuri-galzu was succeeded by his son Mili-sipak, about B.C. 1350, and he by his son Merodach-baladan I., about B.C. 1325. In his time war broke out with Assyria, and Rimmon-nirari, king of Assyria, ravaged Upper Babylonia, and defeated the forces of the Kassu. Assyria now conquered the region of the Khabur, and came down past the junction of that river with the Euphrates to the city of Rapiku, which now formed the border between the two countries.

Merodach-baladan is known only from a fine boundary-stone in the British Museum, on which a grant of land is recorded.

Soon after this another war took place between Assyria and Babylonia, and the king of Assyria defeated Nazi-murudas, king of Babylonia, at the city of Kar-istar-agarsal. No other details of this war are known; and from our broken notice it appears to have been about some question of boundary. A rectification of the frontier took place in favour of Assyria, it being now marked close to the river Turnat.

The name of the Assyrian sovereign who defeated Nazi-murudas is lost; but this may have been connected with the conquest of Babylonia by Tugulti-ninip, king of Assyria. Tugulti-ninip, son of Shalmaneser, ruled over Assyria probably at the beginning of the thirteenth century B.C., and we have the bare record left with respect to him, that he conquered Babylonia, and annexed it to Assyria, ruling under the titles of "king of Assyria" "conqueror of Karduniyas," and "king of Sumir and Akkad." This conquest of Babylonia probably forms an important era in the history, and may be the starting-point of the period of 526 years of Assyrian empire, according to Herodotus and Berosus. The date of the event is supposed to be B.C. 1273, but it must be noticed that all the dates in this part of the history are extremely doubtful, being rough calculations on which Assyrian scholars themselves are not agreed.

The united dominion of Assyria and Babylonia did

not last long, for the Babylonians did not sit quietly under the Assyrian yoke. Soon after the death of Tugulti-ninip, about B.C. 1240, we find the two nations separate and at war; the Assyrians led by Bel-kudur-uzur, and the Babylonians by a king, the first part only of whose name is preserved—this is Vul.... The Babylonian sovereign defeated Bel-kudur-uzur, king of Assyria, and the Assyrian monarch was slain in the battle; after which, perhaps by Babylonian influence, Ninip-pal-esar was raised to the throne of Assyria. The Babylonian monarch made a second expedition to Assyria soon after, about B.C. 1220, in order to capture the capital city Assur; but his camp was attacked by Ninip-pal-esar, and he was forced to retreat to Babylonia.

The history of this period is only known to us from Assyrian sources, no Babylonian texts being known during the thirteenth century B.C.

CHAPTER V.

THE ELAMITES IN BABYLONIA.

Elam or Susiana—Invasions of Babylonia by Kudur-nanhundi and Chedorlaomer—Kudur-Mabuk—Flood at Babylon—Wars between Babylon and Assyria—Nebuchadnezzar I. and Maruduk-nadin-ahi—Seven unknown kings.

THE difficulties in the way of writing a history of Babylonia at present are well shown by our inability to fix with precision the various Elamite invasions of that country. Elam, or Susiana, embraced the country on the east of the river Tigris, including most of the plain south of the mountains, and a considerable district in the mountains, which, on this side, bound the great Euphrates Valley. Elam may be said roughly to have lain to the east of Babylonia, the chief seats of the Susian monarchy being on or near the river Ulai, which may be called the artery from Elam. The Elamites were of a totally different race from the Babylonians; for, while the Babylonians in historic times were Semitic, that is, belonged to the same stock as the Arabs, Jews, and Assyrians, the Elamites were Turanians, and certainly differed in language and religion from their western neighbours.

The Elamites were a restless warlike race, ever ready to take up the sword, and often making attacks upon Babylonia. The country was probably split up into various kingdoms, and only at times subject to a single ruler. The great cities were Shushan, Madaktu, and Hidalu; but there were many others, the seats of local chiefs or kings, only sometimes subject to the power of the king.

The power and influence of Elam are shown by the numerous notices in the great Babylonian work on astrology, where allusions are constantly made to the wars between Babylonia and the Elamites.

One of the Assyrian monarchs, Assurbanipal (B.C. 668–626), gives a curious relation, to the effect that a king of Elam, named Kudur-nanhundi, had invaded Babylonia, and carried away an image of the goddess Nana, which was worshipped in Babylonia; and Assurbanipal appears to state that this event was 1,635 years before his own conquest of Elam. This would give us the date of about B.C. 2280 for the raid of Kudur-nanhundi into Babylonia; but some doubt hangs over the interpretation of the inscription, and it appears likely that this early date may, after all, refer to the original making of the image and not to its captivity. Other mutilated texts appear to mention a raid of Kudur-nanhundi, king of Elam, in the twelfth century B.C.; and another Elamite monarch of the same name sent an army into Babylonia during the reign of Sennacherib.

There is another detached notice of the Elamites in the 14th chapter of Genesis, where we are informed that an Elamite monarch, named Chedorlaomer, that is, Kudur-lagamar, ruled over Babylonia, having under him Amraphel, or Amarpul, king of Shinar, Arioch of Ellasar, and Tidal, or Turgal, king of the Goim (the Gutium of the inscriptions). Kudur-lagamar is said to have ruled over Syria, and part at least of Palestine, for twelve years; and then, on the revolt of the Cities of the Plain, he marched into Palestine, in the fourteenth year, and ravaged a considerable part of the country. We are further told that, on his return, he was defeated by Abraham near Damascus, and lost a considerable portion of his booty. The ordinary marginal chronology of our Bibles places these events about nineteen centuries B.C.: but this date is by no means certain, scholars being very divided in opinion as to the date of Abraham.

There can be no doubt that the 14th chapter of Genesis has preserved a most valuable fragment of Babylonian history, and the names and circumstances of the war so well correspond with what we should expect in early Babylonian history, that it must be considered a serious misfortune that we have not yet been able to fix the exact place and epoch of these events.[1]

Just before the time of Hammurabi, the influence of Elam is again noticed, Simti-silhak and his son Kudur-mabuk, who attained such power in Babylonia, belonging to the north-western part of that country. The Elamite origin of these rulers has been recognized from the time when their names were first discovered, and there has even been some suspicion of a connection between Kudur-mabuk and the Kudur-lagamar, who was contemporary with Abraham.

Our next notice of Elamite influence in Babylonia is from the inscriptions of Esarhaddon, king of

[1] It is possible that Arioch is to be identified with Eri-Aku (as the name of Rim-Agu is also written), the son of Kudur-mabug.—S.

Assyria and Babylonia B.C. 681. He relates that 600 years before his time, or about B.C. 1280, there was war in Babylonia, and one party broke open the treasuries of the gods Bel and Nebo, and sent the gold and silver into Elam. For this it was supposed the vengeance of the gods fell upon Babylon, and one of the great canals, called the Arahtu, or Araxes, broke its banks during a flood, and overwhelmed the city, sweeping away both temples and houses in its irruption. This disaster is said to have so ruined the city, that the inhabitants who escaped went away, carrying their gods with them, and founded a city on another site.

Here again comes a difficulty; such a calamity was quite likely to happen, but at present it is impossible to fit the circumstance into any place in contemporary Babylonian history.

The vigorous rule of the Babylonian monarch who conquered and killed Bel-kudur-uzur, king of Assyria, put a stop for a time to Elamite raids into Babylonia; but after him reigned a king named Zamama-zakir-idina B.C. 1200, under whom they once more commenced. The Elamite king made the usual forays across the border, while, on the other hand, Assur-dayan, king of Assyria, to revenge the late Babylonian invasion of that country, crossed the frontier east of the Tigris, and wasted the region of the river Turnat with fire and sword. During the late wars, the territory near the Lower Zab had been annexed to Babylonia, and the cities here, including Laba, Irriya, and Agarsalu, were captured by the Assyrians and plundered.

Bel-zakir-uzur, the next king of Babylonia, was unfortunate. In his time the Elamites were ruled by Kudur-nanhundi, who is said to have exceeded all his ancestors in his violence and injury to Babylonia. He invaded the country, and swept over it like a flood, leaving a terrible memory of the misfortunes he caused.

Again a change happened: a king, named Nabu-kudur-uzur (Nebuchadnezzar), ascended the Babylonian throne, and soon revived the power of the country. Nebuchadnezzar invaded Assyria three times; of his first expedition no details are known. In his second raid, he did not actually come into contact with the Assyrians, although Assur-ris-ilim, king of Assyria, raised a force to oppose him. The Babylonian monarch meeting some difficulties, burned his baggage, and retreated into his own country. In the third expedition Nebuchadnezzar met the forces of

Assur-ris-ilim, and the Assyrian account states that the Babylonians were defeated with some loss; but there is some slight doubt over these details.

Nebuchadnezzar invaded Elam in revenge for the continual plundering expeditions sent out from that country, and a remarkable circumstance is mentioned with respect to this time. When the king was on the expedition, an enormous comet appeared, the tail of which stretched, like a great reptile, from the north to the south of the heavens.

The revival of the country under Nebuchadnezzar was continued under his successor, Maruduk-nadin-ahi. Maruduk-nadin-ahi invaded South Assyria, and having worsted Tugulti-pal-esar, or Tiglath-pileser, king of Assyria, in battle, captured the city of Hekali, and carried off from there the images of the Assyrian deities, Vul and Sala.

Tiglath-pileser, a monarch of great courage and military ability, did not rest under his defeat. The war was renewed with fury next year, and a battle was fought near the junction of the Suhana with the Lower Zab, in South Assyria. Here Maruduk-nadin-ahi was totally defeated, and the Assyrian monarch, following up his advantage, ravaged the region of the river Turnat; then marching down the Tigris, captured Dur-kurigalzu (Akkerkuf), near Baghdad; from thence he marched to Sippara of Shamas (modern Deyr?), and after capturing that, to Sippara of Anunit (modern Abu-hubba?). From thence he marched in triumph to the capital, Babylon, which also fell into his hands. The whole of Upper Babylonia was wasted in this expedition; and besides these places, Upe, or Opis, on the Tigris, and the region from the river Khabur to Rapiqu were conquered.

In spite of these reverses, the reign of Maruduk-nadin-ahi was on the whole a flourishing one, and several inscriptions of this period are known, giving details of sales of property, showing the prosperity of the country.

The next Babylonian sovereign, Maruduk-sapik-zirrat, made peace with Assur-bel-kala, king of Assyria, about B.C. 1100; but after his death a change of dynasty took place at Babylon, and a new king, whose name is uncertain (perhaps Maruduk-sadu-ni), ascended the throne. The Assyrian monarch was hostile to the new ruler, and made an invasion of Babylonia, in which he does not appear to have gained any advantage.

Nothing is now known of Babylonian history for some time, and in this blank it is probable a fragment of history should be placed, which gives an account of the following seven kings.

Simmas-sipak, son of Iriba-Sin, was the governor or leader of the tribes by the Lake Nedjif. He took the crown, ruled with ability and success for seventeen years, and was buried in the cemetery of Sargon. There is a tablet in the British Museum dated in his twelfth year.

After him came Hea-mukin-ziru, son of Qutmar, who set himself up as king, but was not recognized, and only ruled three months. Kassu-nadin-ahu, son of Sappai, followed; he ruled for six years. These three kings are said to have belonged to the region of the sea (Nedjif Lake), and to have ruled for twenty-three years.

After them came Ulbar-surki-idina, son of Bazi, who reigned for fifteen years. He had been leader of the prefects during the reign of Maruduk-nadin-ahi, and is mentioned as a witness on several legal documents.

To him succeeded his brother, . . . -kudur-uzur, for two years, and then another brother . . . . -Suqamuna, for three months: the reigns of the three amounting, it is said, to twenty years and three months. After the rule of the sons of Bazi, the kingdom fell into the hands of the Elamites, and a monarch of this race ruled for six years; then came another revolution, the account of which is lost.

CONTRACT TABLET.

CHAPTER VI.

THE PERIOD OF THE ASSYRIAN WARS.

Obscure kings—Nabu-pal-idina and Assur-nazir-pal—Disputed succession—Conquests of Shalmaneser—The Chaldees—Ma-ruduk-zakir-izkur—Semiramis—The era of Nabonassar—The Babylonian campaigns of Tiglath-pileser.

A FEW obscure notices are all that remain of the next period of Babylonian history.

A king named Rimmon-pal-idina restored the walls of Nipur, and rebuilt the temple at Kisu.

Rimmon-zakir-uzur was engaged in controversy with Assur-narari and Nabu-dayan, kings of Assyria.

Iriba-maruduk is only known from an inscription on a weight.

Merodach-baladan II., his son, restored the temple of Erech. Sibir invaded Assyria, and burnt the city of Adlil. Nabu-zakir-iskun was at war with Assyria, and during his reign the king of Assyria invaded

Babylonia, capturing several cities along the Tigris; among them Baghdad is now mentioned for the first time.[1]

With these doubtful notices some two hundred years pass, until the time of Nabu-pal-idina, who reigned from about B.C. 880 to 853. During his time the Assyrian power was reviving under Assur-nazir-pal, and the Babylonians felt some alarm at the progress of that conqueror.

When in B.C. 879 Assur-nazir-pal determined to attack the Suhi or Shuites, and Sadadu, prince of Shua, sent to Babylon for aid, Nabu-pal-idina resolved to assist them, in order to check the power of Assyria. Accordingly a Babylonian force marched to the aid of the Shuites, who lived along the river Euphrates, below its junction with the Khabur. The capital city of the Shuites was named Suru; it lay on the left or eastern bank of the Euphrates, and close to the stream. The Babylonian force, largely composed of the Kassi, joined the troops of the Shuites, and both occupied Suru, awaiting the coming of Assur-nazir-pal. The Assyrian monarch passing along by the

[1] This is doubtful. The name of the city may be read Khudadu, as well as Bagdadu.—S.

Khabur to its junction with the Euphrates, and then marching down the Euphrates, arrived at Suru, where he found the Shuites and Babylonians entrenched. Assur-nazir-pal at once attacked the place, and after two days' fighting, carried it by assault. Sadudu, with seventy of his men, threw himself into the Euphrates to save his life, and escaped the hands of the Assyrians. In the city, Assur-nazir-pal captured fifty carriages and their men belonging to Nabu-pal-idina, king of Babylonia, with Zabdan his brother, three thousand troops, and Bel-pal-idina, the leader of the army. Besides these, numbers of the soldiers were slain, and much treasure of all descriptions fell into the hands of the Assyrians.

This disastrous end to his attempt to check the Assyrian power led Nabu-pal-idina to adopt in future a policy of non-intervention; and when next year the whole region of the Khabur and the land of Shua revolted against Assyria, the Babylonian monarch did not interfere.

An agreement was subsequently arrived at, by which the frontiers of Assyria and Babylonia were definitely settled, and a treaty followed between Nabu-pal-idina and Shalmaneser, son of Assur-nazir-pal, king of Assyria.

These boundaries were as follows: on the Euphrates, the city of Rapiqu south of Shua, about latitude 34°; on the east of the Tigris, the line passing along by the cities of Tul-bari; the mounds of Zabdan and Abtani to the cities of Hirimu and Harutu; these places all lying south of the Lower Zab. These lines of boundary were really the traditional limits of the two powers; and although they had fluctuated from time to time, there had been no real advance on either side for the past five hundred years.

About B.C. 853 Nabu-pal-idina died, and was succeeded by his son Maruduk-zakir-izkur; but another claimant for the throne appeared in the person of Maruduk-bel-usati, a brother of the new king, who raised a revolt and seized a considerable part of the country.

Shalmaneser, king of Assyria, who had been on friendly terms with the father of the two contending princes, in B.C. 852 marched into Babylonia to settle the matter. He passed the Lower Zab, and marching to the region of the river Turnat, he captured Me-Turnat and Lahiru.

Next year he went again to Babylonia, B.C. 851, and brought Maruduk-bel-usati to bay in Gananati; here he defeated him, and the Babylonian prince fled to Halman in the mountains east of the Tigris. Here he was followed by the Assyrians and killed, with his principal adherents. After the death of Maruduk-bel-usati, Shalmaneser marched in triumph to Babylon, Borsippa, and Cutha, and offered high sacrifices on the altars there to the chief divinities of the country. Shalmaneser then went to the home of the Chaldees, the region of the lake of Nedjif, called then the sea of Marute. This is the second time the Chaldees are mentioned in the inscriptions, the first notice being a poetical statement of Assur-nazir-pal, B.C. 879, who states that the terror of his soldiers swept over Chaldea.

Of the origin of the Chaldees we know nothing. Some of the early Babylonian dynasties are called Chaldean by Berosus, and we sometimes use the word to designate these early sovereigns; but nothing is really known of the Chaldees at that period, and they are not mentioned in any known document before B.C. 879. They were probably a new race, which had not long appeared in Babylonia; and their being located on the west of Babylonia and in the region of the Persian Gulf, makes it probable that they were immigrants from the part of Arabia lying near the shore of the Persian Gulf. A theory has been propounded that they originally came from North Assyria: this is purely visionary, and is opposed to the evidence of the inscriptions.[1]

In the time of Maruduk-zakir-izkur, the Chaldeans had not possession of Babylonia, but were considered as outlying tribes, governed by their own kings; and they were divided into two principal branches, the Dakkuri, lying west of the Euphrates by Nedjif, and the Ukan or Yakin, lying south-east of these by the Euphrates, extending to the Persian Gulf. Adini, king of the Dakkuri, and Musallim-maruduk, of the Ukani, gave presents as tribute to Shalmaneser in the city of Babylon.

The next monarch known in Babylonia bore the name Maruduk-baladsu-iqbi, and reigned during the time of Samsi-Rimmon, king of Assyria. In his fourth expedition, about B.C 820, this Assyrian monarch marched into Babylonia, and after indulging in the

[1] The Chaldeans are called Caldai on the monuments, a word which cannot be identified with the Casdim of the Old Testament (translated "Chaldeans," or "Chaldees," in our version). The word Casdim is perhaps connected with the Assyrian *casidu*, "conqueror." The Caldai first obtained possession of Babylonia under Merodach-Baladan, B.C. 722, and from that time forward formed so integral a part of the population of the country as to give their name to it.—S.

diversion of a lion-hunt on the way, reached the region of the river Turnat, where he besieged the city of Me-Turnat. The people of this city submitted, and were sent as captives to Assyria; and then, crossing the river Turnat, the Assyrian king attacked and destroyed the city of Garsale and two hundred cities round it. Then, passing Yalman and besieging Dihibina, which submitted, but was hardly treated, three hundred villages round were spoiled; then, marching to Datebir, he destroyed two hundred more places, trampling down the plantations, burning the villages, killing the men, and carrying away the women and valuables. Some of the fugitives fled to Kiribti-alani for shelter; but the Assyrians followed them, and destroyed the city, killing there five hundred men. The fugitives who escaped fled to the city of Dur-papsukul, which was situated in the midst of a stream, and was very difficult to approach. The Assyrians attacked and captured the city, and took four hundred and forty-seven villages, putting to the sword three thousand people, and carrying away about an equal number. Here the Assyrians sacked a palace of the king of Babylonia, and carried away rich spoil. Maruduk-baladsu-iqbi, king of Babylon, in the mean time was preparing to resist this invasion, and collected a miscellaneous army, partly of Babylonians, and partly of mercenaries, from Chaldea, Elam, Zimri, and Aram; these he posted at Ahadada, near Dur-papsukul. Here he was attacked by Samsi-Rimmon, and completely defeated; five thousand of his troops were slain, and two thousand captured; one hundred chariots, two hundred carriages, his pavilion, couch, and his camp also fell into the hands of the victors.

Nothing is known of the fruits of this war, and it is uncertain if the Assyrians reaped any benefit but plunder from the expedition.

A little later in the reign of Samsi-Rimmon, king of Assyria, war was renewed in Babylon. In B.C. 816, the Assyrians marched to Zaratu, and next year again to the region of the Turnat where they took the city of Dur, and celebrated a festival to the great god of that place. In B.C. 814 the Assyrians attacked Ahsana, and in B.C. 813 advanced to Chaldea, then in a final campaign marched to Babylon in B.C. 812.

Unfortunately no details are preserved of these wars, and thus we have no knowledge of the condition of the country and the events which took place. It is apparent, however, that the Assyrians were now gaining ground; and, besides the country open to their inroads, it is probable that they now annexed the region of the river Turnat on the east of the Tigris. At any rate, the boundary between the Zab and Turnat is not mentioned again.

The death of Samsi-Rimmon took place about this time, B.C. 812; and Rimmon-nirari III. ascended the throne of Assyria.

The new king was engaged for several years in expeditions to Syria and Media, and it was not until B.C. 796 that he marched against Babylonia. In this and the next year the town of Dur, which was a frontier town of Babylonia, was the point of attack, no advance being made into the interior of the country. A little later, in B.C. 791, an expedition was made by the Assyrians against a border tribe named the Ituha; these, probably, lay above Hit on the Euphrates.

These three slight expeditions of the Assyrians, which may not have been directed against the Babylonian monarchy, indicate a change of policy, and a period of peace between Babylonia and Assyria. After the long wars of the last reign, the leadership of Assyria had been generally acknowledged, and the Chaldean kings now gave tribute to Assyria.

The wife of Rimmon-nirari, king of Assyria, was

named Sammuramat, or Semiramis; she is supposed by many to be the celebrated queen of that name mentioned by Herodotus, who was said to have built the city of Babylon. Some connection between Assyria and Babylonia is argued on these grounds; but these conclusions are very doubtful, and there is not the slightest proof of any political union between the two countries during this reign. The name of Semiramis may have belonged to several queens, and the celebrated woman of that name probably flourished much earlier.

During the reign of the next Assyrian sovereign, Shalmaneser III., B.C. 783–773, there were three expeditions to Ituha, in B.C. 783, 782, and 777; and in the following reign, that of Assur-dayan, B.C. 773–755, there was one to Gananati, B.C. 771, one to Ituha, B.C. 769, and a second to Gananati, in B.C. 767. No details of these wars are known, and after the last expedition complete darkness comes over the history of Babylonia for twenty years. When the history of Babylonia recommences in B.C. 747, we arrive at a period in which the Assyrian annals are far more complete; and in the canon of the kings of Babylon left by Ptolemy we have the names of the Babylonian rulers from this period down to the end of the kingdom.

According to the canon of Ptolemy, a ruler named Nabonassar commenced his first year at Babylon in B.C. 747, and reigned down to B.C. 734. In the Assyrian inscriptions no mention is made of Nabonassar, but much light is thrown on the condition of the country. In the year B.C. 746 a revolt took place in Calah, which ended in the elevation of Tiglath-pileser to the Assyrian throne, B.C. 745; and the same year the new king, preparing for a more vigorous policy, marched his army against Babylonia.

It appears from the notices of these campaigns that there had been a great decline of the central power in Babylonia, while various tribes of Chaldeans, Arameans, and Arabs had increased in every direction. These tribes now spread all over the country, owning little subjection to Babylon, and encroaching on every side on the settled population. Among them are enumerated the Ituha, Rubuha, Havaran, Luhuatu, Harilu, Rubbu, Rapiqu, Hiranu, Rabili, Naziru, Nabateans, Bagdadites, Hindaru, Hagarenes, and many others. The Chaldeans were now no longer divided into only two tribes; beside the Dakkuri and Yakin, there had arisen the tribes of Silani, Sahala, and Amukkan; and another branch had established themselves at the ancient city of Larak or Larancha.

The original native population of the country appears to have decayed, and the Chaldeans were rapidly taking their place.

The object of the first campaign of Tiglath-pileser was to check the power of the various wandering tribes now overrunning the country. The campaign was conducted through the region of the river Dijaleh, on the east of the Tigris; and from thence the Assyrian monarch crossed the Tigris, and captured Dur-kurigalzu and Sippara of Shamas, together with the smaller cities Kalain, Qurbut, Pahhaz, Kinnipur, and Pazitu. At the close of the expedition, Tiglath-pileser possessed all the region of the Tigris, as low down as Nipur (now Niffer), and appointed military governors to administer the districts; but he does not yet appear to have attacked the west of the country, and all the region of Babylon and the Euphrates remained independent. Numbers of the people conquered in this expedition were carried away by Tiglath-pileser to people the new city Kar-Assur, which he now founded in South Assyria.

The Chaldeans were but little affected by the war in B.C. 745, as their principal seats lay in the west of the country, which this time escaped the Assyrian inroads.

According to Ptolemy's Canon, Nabonassar died

B.C. 734, and was succeeded by Nabius or Nadius, who may be represented by the Nabu-usabsi of the Assyrian inscriptions. This is, however, doubtful, as Nabius probably died B.C. 732, while Nabu-usabsi is mentioned in the next year, B.C. 731, when Tiglath-pileser made his second expedition to Babylonia.

In this expedition, B.C. 731, Tiglath-pileser directed his efforts against the Chaldeans, who had possession of the Euphrates region, the Arameans and Gambuli on the Tigris having been subdued in B.C. 745. Attacked by Tiglath-pileser, the various tribes showed no union, and made no concerted resistance; each kingdom stood on its own defence, and consequently most of them felt the full force of the Assyrian attack.

The first tribe met by Tiglath-pileser was that of the Silani. Nabu-usabsi, king of the Silani, shut himself up in his capital, Sarapanu, where he was attacked by the Assyrians, who captured the place and destroyed it. Nabu-usabsi fell into the hands of Tiglath-pileser, and was impaled in front of his capital. His wife and children, gods and wealth, with 55,000 people, were carried captive. The tribe of Sahala was next attacked; Zakiru of Sahala was captured, and sent in fetters to Assyria. Tiglath-pileser then proceeded against Kinziru, king of the tribe of Amukkan, whose capital city was named Sapiya. Kinziru retired to Sapiya, and was besieged there by Tiglath-pileser. Considerable time had been taken up in the siege and capture of the other towns, and the season was probably now far advanced. This was most probably the reason why Tiglath-pileser, after ravaging the country and destroying the trees, retired without taking the city. While the Assyrian monarch was engaged in the siege of Sapiya, some of the other Chaldean chiefs, fearing that if he captured Sapiya their turn would come next, sent and gave tribute to Tiglath-pileser. These princes were Balasu (Belesys), the chief of the Dakkuri, Nadini, the chief of Larancha, and Merodach-baladan, of the tribe of Yakin, chief of the region of the Euphrates to the Persian Gulf.

Probably about this time Tiglath-pileser formally proclaimed himself king of Babylonia, and in B.C. 730 and 729 he instituted festivals in the principal Babylonian cities in honour of the great gods of the country. These offerings were customary when the kings of Assyria went to Babylon. They are mentioned before in the annals of Shalmaneser II. and Vul-nirari III. At Babylon, Tiglath-pileser took part in the ceremony called taking the hand of Bel, which probably accompanied the accession of a new king.

Here he also made sacrifices to Bel, or Merodach, and his consort Zirat-banit. At Borsippa, he sacrificed to Nebo and his consort Tasmit; and at Cutha, to Nergal and his consort Laz. Offerings were also made in the cities of Kisu, Sippara, Nipur, and Ur. The canon of Ptolemy gives here the two names of Chinzirus and Porus, which represent Kinziru and Pul, their first year in Ptolemy being B.C. 731, and their last B.C. 727.

Some scholars consider that the name of Porus, or Pul, here given among the Babylonian kings, represents Tiglath-pileser, who, about this time, claimed the title of king of Babylon. At the close of the reign of Tiglath-pileser at Nineveh, and of Kinziru and Pul at Babylon, B.C. 727, the canon of Ptolemy gives the name of Ilulæus, or Yugæus, at Babylon, and Shalmaneser at Nineveh. Nothing is known of the connection between these two, and it is probable that Shalmaneser was, during all his short reign, too busily engaged in Palestine to visit Babylonia; but one military report to the king of Assyria connects his name with some events at the city of Dur and the land of Chaldea. It is believed that the difficulties met with by Shalmaneser in Syria led to a revolt on a change of dynasty at Nineveh, Sargon, the new Assyrian monarch, ascending the throne B.C. 722.

CHAPTER VII.

MERODACH-BALADAN AND THE DESTRUCTION OF BABYLON.

Merodach-baladan, the Chaldean, conquers Babylon—Defeated by Sargon—Sargon king of Babylon for five years—Hagisa—Merodach-baladan retakes Babylon—Battle of Kisu—Bel-ibni governor of Babylon—Assur-nadin-sum—Sennacherib's naval expedition to Nagitu—Revolt of Suzub—Elam devastated by the Assyrians—Battle of Khalule—Destruction of Babylon by Sennacherib.

THE circumstances which happened at Nineveh at the time of Sargon's accession to the throne favoured an attempt to snatch Babylonia from the grasp of Assyria, and this was accomplished by Merodach-baladan, one of the most remarkable men in Babylonian history.

He is first heard of in B.C. 731 sending presents of gold and silver, vases of gold, necklaces of gold and pearls, precious woods, robes, spices, oxen, and sheep as presents to Tiglath-pileser to ward off an attack of the Assyrian army.[1]

His territory then lay along the Euphrates, and he had a powerful castle near the river, called Dur-yakin, or the fortress of Yakin, which formed his centre of government. He ruled a people half-traders, half-pirates, and by his activity extended his power until the whole region of the Persian Gulf was under his sway. His next step was to unite all the Chaldean tribes, and then, taking advantage of the change of dynasty at Nineveh, he marched to Babylon, B.C. 722, put an end to the Assyrian dominion, and proclaimed himself king of Babylonia.

Sargon, the new king of Assyria, after crushing the revolt in Palestine, which had impeded his predecessor, marched, B.C. 721, against Babylonia. Merodach-baladan, unable to meet Sargon alone, made alliance with Humba-nigas, the king of Elam; and when Sargon descended against them, he was met by the forces of the Susian king, who had crossed the Elamite frontier to the city of Dur, or Duran.

Here a battle took place, and the Assyrians drove

[1] Merodach-baladan is called the son of Yagina or Yakin, the Yugæus of Ptolemy's Canon.—S.

back the army of Humba-nigas. After which, advancing into Babylonia, Sargon wasted the lands of some of the tribes, but did not come up with Merodach-baladan, or reach Babylon itself. Next year Sargon was forced to march into Syria; and he was engaged in Media, Armenia, Asia Minor, and Palestine down to the year B.C. 711, having no opportunity of renewing his expedition against Babylon.

During this period Merodach-baladan governed Babylonia with ability, and the country was generally prosperous; but expecting an attack from Sargon, he sent, about B.C. 712, an embassy to Hezekiah, king of Judah, to make an alliance with him against Assyria.

The period for this resistance was, however, past. In B.C. 711, Sargon came down on Palestine, and crushed the revolt there, and then prepared to attack Merodach-baladan.

Failing in his projected alliance with Judah, Merodach-baladan sent to Sutur-nanhundi, or Sutruk-nanhundi, king of Elam, and induced him to join in a league against Assyria.

With respect to the origin of his expedition, Sargon tells us that Merodach-baladan, son of Yakin, king of Chaldea, "who, within the sweep of the sea of the rising sun, had his country on the sea and to the flood trusted, the worship and pledges of the great gods forsook, and ceased his presents. Humbanigas, the Elamite, to his aid he had brought, and all the Suti, the people of the desert, he had made hostile; he had prepared war, and the countries of Sumir and Akkad for twelve years against the will of the gods, and Babylon, the city of Bel, he had possessed and controlled."

Both parties in the coming struggle appealed to the same deities, and both accused the other of impiety, while the Babylonian priests stood ready to bless either if victorious.

Merodach-baladan, aware of the coming attack, was not idle. He repaired the fortifications, and collected his army, calling, among others, the tribe of Gambul to garrison the city of Dur-athara, which lay near the river Surappi, on the road of Sargon to Babylon; and he strengthened the fortifications, in the hope that the place would stop the advance of Sargon. To the help of the Gambulai he threw into the city 600 horses and 4,000 troops, and to increase the defence, they pierced the banks of the Surappi, and flooded the region round the city. These precautions were of no avail. Sargon invested the city, and captured it in the evening, taking 18,490 prisoners, with horses, asses, camels, oxen, and sheep. A considerable body of people, under eight chiefs, who had sheltered themselves in the marshes and reed-beds beside the river Ukni, hearing of the capture of the city, were terrified, and sent a present of oxen and sheep to Sargon as a token of submission. The Assyrian monarch rebuilt the city, calling it Dur-Nabu. He appointed a general in command, and directed the payment of an annual tribute of 1 talent 30 manas of silver, a quantity of grain, one ox, and one sheep.

Several other places fell, among them Qarinani, the city of Nabu-uzalla, chief of the Gambulai. Three other tribes, the Hindaru, the Yatbur, and the Puqudu (the Pekod of Jeremiah l. 21), fled in the night, and taking to the water of the river Ukni, made the canal of Umliyas their refuge. Sargon shut them in by building two forts of reeds and mud, and they were starved into a surrender. Yanuqu of Zame, Nabu-uzalla of Aburi, Izmasunu and Haukanu of Nuhani, and Sahali of Ibuli, five chiefs of the Pekod,—Abhata, chief of the Ruhua and Bel-ninu, Samiha, Saphar, and Rapiha, chiefs of the Hindaru, were the leaders who submitted, and their tribute was paid in oxen and sheep, delivered in the city of Athara. Fourteen of the principal cities by the river Ukni were now ravaged, and Sargon then attacked Samhana and Dur-sar, two fortresses of Sutur-nanhundi, king of Elam, which were situated in the district of Yatbur, on the east of the Tigris. Singusibu, the Elamite commander, and 7,520 of the Elamite troops, 12,062 people, with horses, camels, asses, mules, and much spoil, were captured. Up to this time the region of Lahiru had belonged to Elam; now Sargon captured it, and added it to the Assyrian borders; then passing the Elamite cities of Tul-humba, Bube, and Hamanu, in the district of Rasi, he attacked Bit-imbi, and entered it. During this raid into his territories, Sutur-nanhundi, king of Elam, retired with his army to the mountains, fearing to meet the large and well-equipped army brought into his country by Sargon. The motive of the Assyrian monarch was to drive back the Susians, and prevent them from giving aid to Merodach-baladan; and for this purpose he garrisoned the cities he had captured from the Elamites in Yatbur, and held them to protect his rear, while he marched westward across the Tigris to attack Merodach-baladan. Passing over the intermediate country, he crossed to the west of the Euphrates, and took up his head-quarters at Dur-ladini, in the district inhabited by the tribe of Dakkuri. Merodach-baladan, who was then at Babylon, was at once alarmed, and sent rich presents, a couch and a throne of silver, a table, a plate and goblet, all of silver, and a necklace, to Sutur-nanhundi, king of Elam, with urgent requests that he would come to his aid. The Susian monarch, however, had just felt the weight of the Assyrian sword; his borders were ravaged, his frontier forts captured and garrisoned by the troops of Sargon, and he himself had retired to the mountainous district in the east of his dominions for fear of the Assyrians. Under these circumstances, Sutur-nanhundi sent to say that the Assyrian forces blocked his way, and he could not come.

Merodach-baladan now found himself alone, and being a foreigner at Babylon, could not depend upon the people in a siege; he therefore retired at once to the city of Iqbi-Bel, preparatory to a further retreat to Dur-yakin. The judgment of Merodach-baladan was confirmed by the event; for no sooner had he left the city than the priests and people of Babylon and Borsippa sent an embassy, headed by some of the leading men of the city, to invite Sargon to enter.

The Assyrian king then entered Babylon in triumph, and set to work at once to repair the canal which ran from Babylon to Borsippa, and to offer rich sacrifices to the gods of the country. During the advance of the army of Sargon, a tribe named the Hamaran, took advantage of the confusion to plunder. Throwing themselves into the city of Sippara, they issued from it from time to time to ravage the lands of the Babylonians.

Sargon, as soon as he took possession of Babylon, sent a force against them, and besieged the city of Sippara, which he captured, making a severe example of the whole tribe. These operations concluded the campaign, and Sargon prepared to drive Merodach-baladan out of Chaldea. Next year, B.C. 709, in the month Iyyar, the Assyrian monarch started from Babylon and marched towards Iqbi-Bel.

Meanwhile, Merodach-baladan had retreated from Iqbi-Bel, carrying his gods with him, and entering the city of Dur-yakin, near the Euphrates, he called together the tribes who were still faithful to him, and the people of Ur, Erech, Eridu, Larsa, Zarilab, Kisik, and Nimit-laguda, the cities in the south, which still acknowledged his authority; and massing a large army, placed Dur-yakin in a state of defence. With him were the remnants of the tribes which Sargon had conquered—the Gambulai, Pekod, Damun, Ruhua, and Hindaru—and he set his people to work to dig a wide trench, 200 cubits wide (340 feet) and 1½ gurs (30 feet) deep, round the city of Dur-yakin; then opening a channel to the Euphrates, he flooded this ditch, and breaking down the bridges which he had built across it, prepared to resist a siege. Sargon passed his troops across the ditch, and attacked the Chaldeans, who were caught in a net, and defeated with great slaughter. The royal pavilion of Merodach-baladan, his couch of gold, throne of gold, chair of gold, sceptre of gold, chariot of silver, covered carriage of gold, with his other goods, and all his camp fell into the hands of the Assyrians, while the Chaldean monarch, impelled by fear, fled into his citadel with the remnant of his forces. This battle had taken place in the space between the ditch and the city walls; and Sargon now invested the city, which he soon after stormed and captured. Merodach-baladan now submitted, and laid down his sceptre before Sargon, who carried him into captivity, together with his wife, his children, and his treasures.

Thus the whole of Babylonia fell into the hands of Sargon, who set to work to reverse the policy of Merodach-baladan. He expelled the military desert-tribes whom the Chaldean had settled in the Babylonian cities, and everywhere made friends with the priesthood by restoring the rites and offerings of the various gods. Sargon also for some time held his court at Babylon; and while here there came two embassies from opposite sides of the empire to acknowledge the power of the Assyrian monarch. One of these was from Uperi, king of Nituk or Dilmun, a state which is said to have lain thirty kaspu, or about 210 miles, in the sea on the east, being reached through the Persian Gulf. Dilmun has not been identified, and if it were not for the statement of distance, it would be likely to represent the region of the Indus, for it was not the name of a small, obscure place, but of a region known from remote times, and always spoken of as the eastern boundary on the sea.[1]

The second embassy came from the West, from the seven kings of Yaha, a district of Yatnan, a place said to be seven days' sail in the Mediterranean. This embassy is usually supposed to have come from Cyprus; but this island appears too close to the coast to require such a voyage.

Sargon reigned at Babylon after his conquest of Merodach-baladan for five years, and died B.C. 705.

[1] Dilmun, or rather Dilvun, is probably the modern Bunder-Dellim.—S.

During the reign of Sargon, some troubles took place from the leaning of the Chaldean tribes to the cause of Merodach-baladan. Partial revolts happened; but these were easily repressed, and Sargon remained on the throne until his death.

On the death of Sargon, his son Sennacherib became king of Assyria, on the 12th day of Ab, B.C. 705; and it is supposed that a brother of the king was made ruler at Babylon. There is, however, as usual, considerable obscurity as to the history and succession here. It appears from the Chronicle of Eusebius, that after the death of the brother of Sennacherib the Babylonians raised to the throne Hagisa, or Akises; and Merodach-baladan, escaping from the Assyrians, murdered the new ruler after a reign of one month, and again mounted the Babylonian throne, B.C. 704. This defection of Babylon called up Sennacherib, the new Assyrian monarch, and he assembled his army to march to Babylon.

The Assyrians marched into the country, and crossed the Tigris in the direction of the capital, meeting little opposition on their way until they came to Kisu (Hymer), about nine miles east of Babylon, where Merodach-baladan had drawn up his forces. Here a battle took place, and the Babylonian forces were routed, the Chaldean monarch taking refuge in flight. It is probable that Babylon at this time was not prepared to stand a siege, and therefore Merodach-baladan at once hastened to the south to take refuge in the reeds and swamps which in all ages have formed the shelter of political refugees. Here in the district of Guzuman he hid himself safely from his foes, while the Assyrians searched the reeds and marshes in vain to find him.

Immediately after the battle of Kisu, Sennacherib entered Babylon and plundered the palace, carrying away everything. A like fate awaited all the other cities within reach. According to one record, 89 cities and 820 villages were destroyed, while another gives 76 cities and 420 villages. Among these few names remain; but Sarrapanu and Larancha are mentioned, and Erech (Warka), Nipur (Niffer), Kisu (Hymer), Harris-kalama[1] (near Hymer), and Cutha (Ibrahim) are given as seats of the Chaldeans. After the country within reach of the Assyrian army had been conquered and ravaged, Sennacherib set to work to reconstruct the government. With him he had a young man named Bel-ibni, son of a Babylonian

[1] Rather Kharsak-kalama, "the mountain of the world," so called from the name of its principal temple.—S.

officer. He had grown up in the palace of the king of Assyria, and was now raised by Sennacherib to the throne of Babylonia, his appointment dating B.C. 703. It appears that a further campaign was necessary in this year to chastise the various nomad tribes wandering over the country. It is said that at the close of these operations 208,000 people, with multitudes of flocks and herds, were carried captive to Assyria. Nabu-bel-zakri, governor of Hararti, was the only ruler who voluntarily submitted; and he, probably fearing a visit from the Assyrian army, sent rich presents to Sennacherib. The work of spoiling being finished, the Assyrian monarch rebuilt the city of Hirimmu, which he had destroyed, and appointed a tribute from it of one ox, ten sheep, ten homers of wine, and twenty homers of first-fruits, as an offering to the Assyrian gods.

Sennacherib returned to Assyria in B.C. 703, leaving the government in the hands of Bel-ibni, and appointing a force to watch for Merodach-baladan. The Chaldean prince, finding the Assyrian garrisons too strong for him, and despairing of regaining his Babylonian throne, called together his adherents, and collecting the images of his gods, resolved to lead a Chaldean colony to a new district on the Persian

Gulf. Taking ship with his adherents, he abandoned the country where he had struggled for thirty years against the Assyrian power, and carried his people down the Persian Gulf to the district of Nagitu, on the Asiatic shore, within the territory of Elam. Here, an exile from his native land, Merodach-baladan died; but he left several sons, destined to continue their father's work and continue his opposition to Assyria. After the departure of Merodach-baladan to Nagitu, another Chaldean chief arose, Suzub, son of Gahul, who collected a band of followers at the city of Bittut, in the marsh district near the mouth of the river Euphrates, and defied the power of the Assyrians. To punish him, Sennacherib organized a second expedition to Chaldea, in B.C. 700, and defeated Suzub, who escaped and hid himself. Then turning to Bit-yakin, the district of Merodach-baladan, the Assyrian army ravaged the place, carrying captive those who had not emigrated with Merodach-baladan. The rule of Bel-ibni was probably unsatisfactory to Sennacherib, for the Assyrian monarch, at the close of the expedition, gave the government of the country to his own eldest son, Assur-nadin-sum, who commenced his reign B.C. 700. The new Chaldean establishment at Nagitu, on the Persian Gulf, was beyond the reach of the Assyrians, and independent of their influence, while it formed a fresh focus of Chaldean independence. Sennacherib, therefore, formed the design of subjugating this region; and unable to reach it by land through the hostile country of Elam, he directed a fleet to be prepared, with a view to attack the emigrants from the sea. Two stations were formed, one at Nineveh, on the Tigris, the other at Tul-barsip (Biradjik),[1] on the Euphrates; and Tyrian workmen were employed to build there large vessels fit for a sea voyage, and crews were selected of Tyrians, Zidonians, and Greeks. The Tigris being in places shallow on account of the dams and rapids, the vessels built at Nineveh were floated empty down to the city of Upe (Opis), and there they were passed into a navigable canal, called the Arahtu or Araxes, and were drawn through this to the river Euphrates, in the Chaldean region; here the troops and stores were waiting, and the vessels were loaded. The fleet now dropped down the river to Bab-salimiti, on the right bank at the mouth of the Euphrates, where Sennacherib went on shore and pitched his camp. The troops had

[1] Tul-barsip is rather opposite Carchemish, the modern Jerablus. It is the Barsampse of Ptolemy. Biradjik represents the "Birtu of the Arameans" of the Assyrian inscriptions.—S.

been five days descending the river, until they reached the shore of the Persian Gulf at Bab-salimiti. At the place where the river issued into the sea, Sennacherib made a great festival in honour of Hea, the presiding deity of the ocean. Images of fishes and vessels, made of gold, were carried out to sea and dropped with great ceremony into the ocean by the Assyrian monarch, while victims and libations were offered to Hea, the Assyrian Neptune. It being supposed that the gods were propitiated, the expedition sailed out to sea and made for the Persian coast, where the district of Nagitu was situated. Here they came to the mouth of the river Ulai, which formed the artery of Nagitu, and in the vicinity of which the cities colonized by the Chaldeans were situated. It is quite evident that since the time of Sennacherib considerable changes have taken place in the geography of this region; the soil rapidly accumulates at the head of the Persian Gulf, and now the mouth of the Ulai no longer opens into the sea, but discharges itself into the Euphrates.

On the arrival of the Assyrian fleet at the mouth of the Ulai, they found the Chaldeans gathered to receive them. The colonists inhabited the cities of Nagitu and Nagitu-dihibin, and they called to their assistance the people of Hilmu, Bellatu, and Hupapanu drawing up their forces on the flat fronting the Ulai. The Assyrian troops were disembarked, and attacked with fury the Chaldeans and their allies, routing them and pursuing them to their cities, which they captured and spoiled. The people were captured in large numbers, and with their goods and cattle forced into the Assyrian ships and sent over to the city of Bab-salimiti to Sennacherib.

While this expedition was away at the Persian Gulf, Suzub, who had escaped during the former war, raised a force in the rear of Sennacherib, and the king of Elam, who had hitherto only given secret help to the Babylonians, now marched his army to Babylon, and with them came numbers of the Chaldean emigrants returning to their country. The Elamite and Chaldean forces captured Babylon, and proclaimed Suzub king; but reinforcements being sent to the Assyrian army, they turned and defeated the rebels, capturing Suzub, who was sent bound to Nineveh.

At this time one of the parties fell upon the city of Erech, and plundered it, carrying away the images of the gods; but the notice of this event is so ambiguous, that it is uncertain if it was the Assyrian or the Elamite army which plundered the temples. The direct interference of the Elamites at Babylon during these operations, and their constant hostility to Assyria, now led to a war between the two countries. Sennacherib, in resolving to attack the Elamites, was also influenced by a desire to recover a small portion of Assyrian territory near Duran, which had been attacked and captured by the Elamites just before the close of the reign of Sargon. Here the Elamites had taken the two cities of Bit-hairi and Raza, and this loss had not been recovered. About B.C. 697, the Assyrian monarch set out with a large army to make war with Elam, and after recovering the lost district he went on to attack the Elamite cities, which he captured and burned one after another. Thirty-four larger cities, and numerous smaller villages, were destroyed, and the Assyrian records relate that the smoke of these conflagrations rose like a cloud, and obscured the face of the heavens.

During this destruction of his cities, Kudur-nanhundi, the Elamite king, did not dare to meet Sennacherib in the field; but fearing for his own safety, he caused his people to retire into the other cities, and he himself left Madaktu, his capital, and fled into the mountains to Hidalu. Everything now seemed at the mercy of the Assyrian king, who was carrying fire and sword through the country, and sparing nothing in his progress. The sudden setting in of winter rendered the roads impassable, and by stopping the Assyrian monarch's intended march against the capital, Madaktu, put an end to this war of destruction, which had been carried on with a barbarity seldom seen even then.

Brought to a halt by the snow and rain, Sennacherib reluctantly turned and retraced his steps to Assyria; but the Elamites did not easily forget his invasion; within three months their king was dead, and they raised to the throne his brother Umman-minan, a man of a more energetic disposition.

Meanwhile, Suzub had escaped from confinement, and meeting with numerous other fugitives, all eluding the Assyrian governors, he again raised a revolt, and took to the marshes for protection. Here he was pursued by the Assyrians, and so hunted, that he fled into Elam to Umman-minan, the king of that country. Elam at once became a centre for the Chaldean refugees; and Suzub, collecting a number of these, came to Babylon, where the people again opened their gates to him, and by general consent the Assyrians were expelled from the country, and Suzub was once more raised to the throne.

Aware of his inability to hold the throne alone, Suzub broke open the sacred treasures of Bel at Babylon, Nebo at Borsippa, and Nergal at Cutha, and sent the gold and silver as a present to Umman-minan, king of Elam, saying: "Gather thy army, collect thy camp, to Babylon come and strengthen our hands, for a master of war art thou." Umman-minan and his people were equally ready to make war with Assyria, and to avenge the ravages of the Assyrian army during Sennacherib's late campaign, and calling to his standard all the tribes subject to Elam, he took the road to Babylon. An immense host now gathered at this city, consisting of Elamites, Persians, people of Anzan, Pasiru, Ellipi, Yazan, Lagapri, Harzunu, Dummuq, Sulai, Samuna, Adini, Amukkan, Silan, Sahala, Larancha, Lahiru, Pekod. Gambul, and other tribes. Umman-minan and Suzub marched out from Babylon, about B.C. 696, feeling strong enough to meet Sennacherib in the open field. They therefore posted their troops at Halule, on the Tigris, to check the Assyrian monarch before he overran the heart of the country.

Sennacherib advanced to Halule eager to meet the rebels, and joined battle with them, utterly routing their troops. The chiefs of the Elamites and Babylonians had gone out to the battle richly adorned, with arms inlaid with gold, bracelets and rings of gold, riding in chariots plated with silver; and most of these trappings fell into the hands of the Assyrians. The Babylonian army gathered at Halule must have been very numerous, for the Assyrians count the slain at the incredible number of 150,000 men. We are informed, however, that the pursuit and slaughter lasted for four hours after sunset. A multitude of prisoners and heaps of spoil remained with the victors, several of the chiefs, including Nabu-zakir-iskun a son of Merodach-Baladan, falling into the hands of Sennacherib.

The disastrous battle of Halule closed for that year operations in Babylonia. There was a long march to Babylon; the season was probably late, and the Assyrian army crippled, and encumbered with spoil. These reasons probably determined the close of the campaign; but next year Sennacherib once more marched out, resolved this time to make an example of Babylon. This was about B.C. 695. Suzub and Umman-minan, after the battle of Halule, had escaped to their respective countries, and when Sennacherib again invaded Babylonia there was no attempt at opposition in the open field; he advanced at once to Babylon, and appeared before the city, which was ill-prepared to resist him. The fortifications were stormed and captured, and the whole city given up to spoil. Suzub, with part of his family, fell into the hands of Sennacherib, who sent them to Assyria; the treasures of the city were plundered by the soldiers, the images of the gods were brought out of the temples and broken up, the houses were pulled down and burned, the walls were levelled, the temples overturned, and the towers thrown down; the city was levelled, as far as the fury of the Assyrian monarch could do it, and the great canal, called Araxes, was filled up with the ruins.

CHAPTER VIII.

THE RULE OF THE ASSYRIANS.

The successors of Assur-nadin-sum—Nabu-zir-napisti-esir—Babylon rebuilt by Esarhaddon—Succeeded by his son Saul-mugina—Wars with Elam—Revolt of Babylonia—Crushed by Assur-bani-pal—Saul-mugina perishes in the flames of his palace—Nabopolassar appointed governor—He marries the daughter of Cyaxares of Media—The fall of Nineveh.

VERY little is known of the history of Babylonia for some years after its destruction by Sennacherib. Suzub again escaped from captivity, and opposed Sennacherib; but he was ultimately killed by a fall from his horse. Assur-nadin-sum, son of Sennacherib, who had reigned whenever the Assyrians held Babylon, died B.C. 694, and, according to Ptolemy, was succeeded by Rigebel; after whom came Mesesi-mardochus, B.C. 693 to 689. From this time, not even the names of the Babylonian rulers appear, and the city remained in obscurity until the reign of Esarhaddon.

During this time, a son of Merodach-baladan, named Nabu-zir-napisti-esir, took possession of his father's original territory near the Persian Gulf; and after strengthening himself there, he aspired to the dominion of the whole of Babylonia. After the murder of Sennacherib his sons disputed the crown, and taking advantage of the confusion, the Chaldean prince, in B.C. 681, marched against the city of Ur (Mugheir), then governed by Ningal-idina, who was faithful to the Assyrian empire. Having failed to separate the governor of Ur from the interest of the Assyrians, he besieged the city, and when Esarhaddon, having gained a decisive victory over his brothers, was proclaimed king at Nineveh, Nabu-zir-napisti-esir disregarded his accession, and continued his hostilities against Assyria. Esarhaddon, hearing of this, ordered the Assyrian generals who were stationed in Babylonia to march against him; and unable to meet their forces, the Chaldean prince fled into Elam, the old refuge of his father. The reign of Esarhaddon had opened with great promise, and he had assumed the crowns of both Assyria and Babylonia. The Elamites now appeared disinclined to quarrel with him, and did not take up the cause of the son of their old ally, Merodach-baladan. Nabu-zir-napisti-esir thus found Elam an insecure refuge, and soon after his arrival there was treacherously murdered. His brother, Nahid-Maruduk, who had followed his fortunes and shared his flight to Elam, when he saw the death of Nabu-zir-napisti-esir, alarmed for his own safety, fled out of the country, and threw himself upon the mercy of Esarhaddon. The Assyrian monarch received him favourably, accepting his homage, and appointing him to the government of the district of the sea-coast, which his brother had forfeited by rebellion.

As soon as he had settled his affairs in Assyria, Esarhaddon came in person to Babylon (January, B.C. 680), and set to work to restore the city, which had been ruined by the late wars. He rebuilt the great temples and towers, restored the fortifications, and brought back the captive images of the gods. Under the fostering care of Esarhaddon, Babylon soon again became a great city, and the rival of Nineveh. During the depression of Babylon, in the latter part of the reign of Sennacherib, the chief of the Chaldean tribe of Dakkuri, whose home was on the edge of the desert west of Babylon, had encroached upon the grounds of the people of Babylon and Borsippa. These people Esarhaddon checked, and put a stop to their inroads. He seized Samas-ibni, their king, and burned him, as a punishment, and set up in his place a chief named Nabu-usallim. Soon after this the new chief sent an urgent despatch to Esarhaddon, because the marsh tribes had gathered in Bit-amukkan, and endeavoured to renew the depredations which had been carried on in the time of Samas-ibni. He prays the king to send to Sadu, governor of Amukkan, and check these raids. Subsequently Esarhaddon was informed that Nabu-usallim, whom he had raised to office, was endeavouring to purchase horses; and the governor of Babylon, for Esarhaddon, stated that the governor of the Dakkuri desired to raise a force to attack the Assyrian army, and renew the raids of Samas-ibni, in consequence of which he, as viceroy of the king of Assyria, forbade the sales in the name of Esarhaddon.

In the same letter the governor of Babylon informs Esarhaddon of the arrival of Bel-basa, son of Bunanu, at Babylon and Borsippa, from which cities he went to the land of the tribe of Dakkuri. Bel-basa was chief of the tribe of Gambul, which lived in the marshes by the Tigris, close to the Elamite frontier. He was induced to submit to Esarhaddon; and in consideration of his alliance, Esarhaddon assisted him to build the city of Sapi-Bel, in the marshes, which he was to hold for Esarhaddon as a frontier fortress against the Elamites.

Some time later, Umman-aldas being on the throne of Elam, his two brothers, Urtaki and Te-umman, proposed to him that he should break the peace with Esarhaddon, and make an expedition into Chaldca against the king of Assyria. This he refused to do, and they then murdered him, setting up in his place Urtaki, his next brother. The new king was wiser on his accession than to follow his own former council, and made friendly advances to Esarhaddon. Te-umman, the youngest brother, who appears to have been a determined foe of Assyria, was not satisfied with this policy, and sent an agent of his own, named Zineni, into Chaldea, to endeavour to raise a revolt in favour of Nabu-diim, a son of the late Chaldean ruler. The people were, however, satisfied with their government, and returned answer that Nahid-Maruduk was their lord, and that they were subjects of the king of Assyria. Esarhaddon continued to reign in peace over Babylon for thirteen years, his rule being only diversified by these small intrigues and domestic events; and on his death in B.C. 668, he left the government of Babylon to his younger son, Saul-mugina, the elder son, Assur-bani-pal, being already installed as king of Assyria.[1]

Peace continued in Babylonia under the rule of Saul-mugina, who answers to the Saosduchinos of Ptolemy and the Sammughes of Polyhistor.

This general quiet was, however, broken after about ten years, by Urtaki, king of Elam. He had been on good terms with Esarhaddon, and afterwards with his sons; but suddenly changing his policy, he persuaded Bel-basa, king of the Gambulai, and some other local chiefs, to join him in hostility against Assur-bani-pal and Saul-mugina. Urtaki then, with these chiefs in his train, made an irruption into Babylonia, and spreading his troops over the country, gave it up to plunder. Saul-mugina, who was in Babylon, was alarmed at this inroad, and sent at once to ask the aid of his brother Assur-bani-pal, king of Assyria. At this time, although Saul-mugina was king of Babylon, he was tributary and subject to his elder brother,

[1] It was while Esarhaddon was holding his court at Babylon that Manasseh of Judah was brought there captive, according to 2 Chronicles xxxiii. 11. The character and rule of Esarhaddon seem to have been mild, and the release of Manasseh from captivity is paralleled by other similar acts of clemency upon his part.—S.

Babylon being dependent upon Nineveh. Assur-bani-pal himself appointed the provincial governors in Babylonia. He had his own garrisons and commanders, and his generals reported to himself instead of to his brother. Besides this, he repaired the Babylonian temples, and made offerings at the various shrines in his own name, thus having the priesthood immediately connected with himself. The active control of affairs being thus in the hands of the king of Assyria, Assur-bani-pal responded to the appeal of his brother, and after sending an officer to report to himself on the Elamite raid, he suddenly moved a force into Babylonia, and, coming up with Urtaki before he could retreat into Elam with his spoil, inflicted upon him a defeat and drove him across the border.

This war led to a succession of contests with Elam, which belong rather to the history of Assyria than to that of Babylonia. The result of these expeditions was, that Assur-bani-pal conquered Elam, and set upon the throne of that country Umman-igas, a son of Urtaki, who engaged to pay tribute to Assyria.

The Elamites, who were a brave, warlike race, were restless under the yoke of Assyria; and Saul-mugina, king ot Babylon, was also tired of his subordinate position. General disaffection spread over Chaldea, Arabia, Syria, and Palestine; while Psammetichus, king of Egypt, had revolted, and, expelling the Assyrians from that country, in alliance with Gyges, king of Lydia, made war against Assur-bani-pal. The moment seemed propitious for a general revolt, and the Assyrian monarch, foreseeing that trouble was coming, issued a proclamation to the Babylonians, dated on the 23rd day of the month Iyyar, in the eponymy of Assur-dur-uzur about B.C. 650. In this document he reminds them of the benefits he had given them, and of the close brotherhood between Assyria and Babylonia.

Saul-mugina at that time meditated a revolt; but to mask his proceedings he sent an embassy to Nineveh, to assure his brother of his fidelity, and to deceive the Assyrian monarch until his preparations were completed. The first object of the Babylonian monarch was to seek allies, and his attention was naturally turned to Elam. Saul-mugina, following the example of several former rulers, broke open the treasuries of Bel at Babylon, Nebo at Borsippa, and Nergal at Cutha, and sent the gold and silver as a present to Umman-igas, king of Elam, in payment for his assistance; and the two monarchs made an agreement to make war against Assur-bani-pal. In Chaldea they were supported by Nabu-bel-zikri, the grandson of Merodach-Baladan, who ruled the sea-coast, by Sin-tabni-uzur, son of Ningal-idina, governor of Ur, by Mannu-ki-babili of Dakkuri, by Hea-mubasa of Amukkan, by Nadan of Pekod, and by various subordinate chiefs. Vahta, king of Arabia, hearing that the Babylonians and Elamites were bent on revolt, sent and made alliance with them, hoping, if the revolt were successful, to gain possession of Palestine and Syria for himself. Vahta raised two forces, one of which he led into Palestine and marched through Edom, Moab, the Hauran, and Hamath, where his progress was stopped by the Assyrian generals, who defeated him and drove him back to his own country. The other force he placed under the control of two chiefs, Aimu and Abiyateh, and sent them to Babylon to draw off the attention of the Assyrians by assisting Saul-mugina at Babylon. Assur-bani-pal, who had received the embassy from his brother with great honour and ceremony, and had feasted them in Nineveh, was suddenly awakened by the breaking out of the revolt; Elam, Babylonia, and Arabia in concert throwing oft the Assyrian yoke.

The king of Elam marched his army into Babylonia,

and the Arabians joined the confederates at Babylon. The combined forces then attacked the Assyrian garrisons, and everywhere expelled the officers of Assur-bani-pal. Saul-mugina chose four cities for military centres: Sippara, Babylon, Borsippa, and Cutha. These he fortified, and prepared to resist a siege, as his brother was gathering a force to reconquer the country.

Before, however, the Assyrians reached the scene, divisions appeared among the insurgents. As soon as Umman-igas, king of Elam, had sent his army to Babylon, his son Tammaritu made a conspiracy against him, and, raising a force, defeated the royal troops. Capturing his father in the battle, he cut off his head, and sent it to Assur-bani-pal. After this, Tammaritu, who had assumed the crown of Elam, was induced by the Babylonians to assist them, and he marched into their country with his army.

Assur-bani-pal was now advancing, and his forces, under the leadership of a general named Bel-ibni, defeated the confederates, and, overrunning the open country, shut them up in the four cities, Babylon, Borsippa, Cutha, and Sippara. When Tammaritu had gone to Babylonia, Inda-bigas, one of his servants, set up as king in Elam, and, the people going over to his side, Tammaritu found himself cut off from his own country. Tammaritu, with the Assyrian army on one side, and Inda-bigas on the other, was in a great strait, and taking flight with some of his friends, he found his way to the sea-coast, where he took ship and tried to escape. The vessel in which Tammaritu sailed was, however, soon afterwards caught in a storm and driven back on the coast, and Tammaritu, being ill, was carried on shore, where he took refuge in the marshes; but on receiving a promise of protection from Assur-bani-pal, he surrendered to the Assyrians.

Meanwhile the Assyrian generals were crushing the Babylonian revolt; the strongholds successively fell, and Babylon, the last hope of the rebels, was closely besieged. Famine and pestilence, the fruits of war, were desolating the country, while the Assyrians were completing its ruin.

In the year B.C. 648 Babylon fell, and Saul-mugina, finding that the city was captured, set fire to his palace, and perished in the flames. After the fall of Babylon, the Assyrians proceeded to punish the smaller chiefs who had aided in the revolt; but one of the most active of these, Nabu-bel-zikri, a grandson of Merodach-Baladan, who ruled the region of the sea-coast, escaped from the officers of Assur-bani-pal, and fled to Elam, to the court of Inda-bigas. Inda-bigas, finding the Babylonian revolt had failed, desired to make his peace with Assur-bani-pal, and sent an embassy to Assyria to propitiate the Ninevite monarch. Assur-bani-pal met the envoy with a demand for the surrender of Nabu-bel-zikri, the grandson of Merodach-Baladan, then a refugee at the court of Inda-bigas, and threatened to invade Elam, and waste it with fire and sword if this demand was not complied with. Before the return of the messenger with this message, Inda-bigas was dead. Umman-aldas, an Elamite commander, had revolted against him, and killed him and his family, in his turn ascending the Elamite throne.

Assur-bani-pal now sent an embassy to the new monarch, to demand the surrender of the Chaldean prince, and Umman-aldas received the envoys of the Assyrian monarch.

Nabu-bel-zikri, now fearing that he should be delivered up by the king of Elam to Assur-bani-pal, called on his armour-bearer to despatch him, and the two ran each other through with their swords. Umman-aldas took the body of Nabu-bel-zikri and the head of his armour-bearer and delivered them to the messengers of Assur-bani-pal, who carried them to Assyria.

The death of Nabu-bel-zikri extinguished the family of Merodach-Baladan, and put an end to the trouble and danger to Assyria arising from their constant efforts to shake off the Ninevite yoke.

Babylonia now enjoyed a quiet of some years under the reign of Assur-bani-pal; but the condition of the country at this time is uncertain. It is supposed that trouble arose on the death of Assur-bani-pal, B.C. 626, and that a claimant named Bel-zakir-iskun set himself up as king. It is certain that at this time there was a revolt of some sort, and the Assyrian monarch sent a general named Nabu-pal-uzur (Nabopolassar) to subdue it. Nabopolassar, after reconquering the country, was rewarded by the Assyrian monarch with the crown of Babylonia. Nabopolassar was a man of genius and ambition, and while Assyria, nominally the governing state, was fast decaying, raised Babylonia to a high pitch of power and prosperity. The fall of Assyria was now imminent. The upper provinces had all been ravaged by the Scythians, and a new and powerful state had arisen on the east of the empire in Media, now ruled by Cyaxares; while Babylonia was being reorganized under Nabopolassar and the Egyptians were laying siege to Ashdod in the west. Cyaxares having determined on the conquest of

Assyria, Nabopolassar sent and offered to make an alliance with him for this purpose, the treaty to be cemented by the marriage of Amuhia or Amytis, the daughter of Cyaxares,[1] with Nabu-kudur-uzur or Nebuchadnezzar, son of Nabopolassar. This treaty probably included also the king of Egypt, for he assisted in the war against Assyria, marching up through

[1] It is very probable that some mutilated tablets discovered by Mr. Smith refer to Cyaxares and the closing days of the Assyrian monarchy. The writing upon them is extremely bad, and they seem to be rough copies hastily executed, and never carefully copied out again. The name of the Assyrian king for whom they were written is Esar-haddon, which may be compared with the name Saracus, assigned to the last monarch of Nineveh by classical writers. We learn from them that Kaztariti king of the Kar-kassi ("the fortress of the Kassi," perhaps), had allied himself with Mamitarsu, the chief of the Medes, the Kimmerians, the Minnians of Lake Van, and the people of Saparda (the Sepharad of Obad. 20), on the Black Sea, and invaded Assyria. Many of the Assyrian cities were taken, and the King of Nineveh ordered a fast of one hundred days and nights to the gods, in order to avert the danger with which the empire was threatened. It was at this crisis, when the enemy was hourly expected to attack Nineveh itself, that the tablets were composed. The predecessor of Nabopolassar at Babylon was Kandalanu, the Kineladanos of Ptolemy, whose 20th year has been found on a contract-tablet. Bel-zakir-iskun did not reign at all in Babylonia.—S.

Palestine to Carchemish on the Euphrates, which he captured.

The account of the siege and fall of Nineveh, and the extinction of the Assyrian empire, will be found in the "History of Assyria," pp. 189–191. No trustworthy history of this period from any ancient source is known, and one difficulty in the case is, to know how to choose between what is probable and what is unlikely in the various notices which have come down to us.

CHAPTER IX.

THE EMPIRE OF NEBUCHADNEZZAR.

Rise of the Babylonian Empire—Egypt and Media—Nebuchadnezzar, his conquests and buildings—Destruction of Jerusalem —Invasion of Egypt—Siege of Tyre—The kingdom of Lydia —Babylon adorned—Character of Nebuchadnezzar—Evil-Merodach, his murder—Nergalsharezer.

AFTER the fall of Assyria, a natural division of the territories of the departed empire was made. The Median provinces and the north of Assyria as far as Cilicia, fell to Cyaxares of Media; the south of Assyria and part of Arabia fell to Babylon, the western boundary of Nabopolassar being the Upper Euphrates. All west of Carchemish and south of Cilicia was joined to Egypt.

It was evident that the division was only provisional, and could only last until the three powers could determine in conflict their relative strength · and accordingly, after about three years, the whole arrangement was overturned by the action of Nabopolassar, king of Babylon.

The overthrow of the Assyrian empire marks a great epoch in the history of the world; it is the indication of a coming change, which swept away the old despotism and base idolatry of Western Asia, and brought in the era of a purer and nobler faith. The king of Babylon and Pharaoh of Egypt assisted in the work of dismembering the expiring empire; but events they little foresaw were ripening, and they were really exchanging for their countries the familiar yoke of Assyria for another and sterner rule, under which their political existence would be crushed.

The great event of this age is the rise of the Medo-Persian power, which showed a remarkable superiority to the empires which preceded it, by a superior system of government, and better military discipline. Its dominion, within a century, extended to the east and west far beyond the greatest limits ever reached by former powers. The complete triumph of the Aryans was, however, delayed by the rise of the reviving Babylonian empire. The brilliant genius of Nabopolassar and his son Nebuchadnezzar made Babylon for the time the centre of the political world. This impetus, due to individual ability, quickly failed, and only left Babylonia a richer and more tempting prize for the rising power of Persia. The fall of Nineveh and sudden extinction of the Assyrian power was followed by a pause in the events then so rapidly hurrying along. Although the hammer of the earth was broken, it seemed for the moment as if there was no state able to take the mantle of the departed empire. The smaller states were now independent, while on the ruins of the Assyrian monarchy stood three powers, apparently equally balanced and equally reluctant to disturb their neighbours.

Egypt on the west was now a great state. Its king held court in Northern Syria, and its soldiers encamped by the banks of the river Euphrates. All the country west of this great natural boundary acknowledged the sway of Pharaoh Necho, the extent of whose empire rivalled the dominions of Egypt in her most palmy days, under the great Thothmes and Rameses of the eighteenth and nineteenth dynasties.

On the south, Babylonia had attained a power which she had not possessed for several centuries: the south of Assyria and the region of the Khabur were added to her empire, and whatever culture and advancement Assyria had possessed had at once gravitated towards Babylon. On the north and east Media had risen within a few years from a condition of division and lawlessness to a compact and powerful monarchy; and the empire of Cyaxares, king of Media, extended from the river Halys, in Asia Minor, to the east of Persia.

There was a mutual agreement between the three powers, and the marriage of the son of the king of Babylon with the daughter of the king of Media assured the peace between these states; besides which, all had so recently acquired their possessions that much organization was necessary before any further extension of them could be made.

It seems that the first power to recover was Babylon. Nabopolassar was active from the first, and organized his new possessions so as to be quickly ready for war; and then, as generally happens, a pretext for hostilities was soon found by one who was looking out for it.

Some discussion arose with Necho, king of Egypt, probably about the rights or boundaries of the Egyptians and Babylonians, and in B.C. 605 war was declared between the two powers. Nabopolassar was now too old and infirm for active operations in the field; and being anxious to prosecute the war with vigour, placed his troops under command of his eldest son, Nebuchadnezzar, a young man of great promise. The Egyptian army meanwhile lay idly at Carchemish, on the Upper Euphrates, Necho not having the judgment to prepare against his young antagonist.

Nebuchadnezzar advanced to Carchemish, and attacked and routed the Egyptian army there, gaining by this movement the control of all Syria. The Egyptians appear to have had no reserves, and the Babylonians marched through Syria and Palestine unopposed, receiving the submission in turn of all the petty princes as far as the borders of Egypt.

Among these tributaries was Jehoiakim king of Judah, who had been set on the throne by Necho, but who was now forced to submit to the Babylonian yoke.

While Nebuchadnezzar was absent in Syria his father, Nabopolassar, died, and Nebuchadnezzar hastened back to Babylon to assume the government. The Babylonian army now returned laden with the spoils of the west and the tribute of Syria, and Babylon assumed the position of metropolis of the world.

Soon after Nebuchadnezzar had returned to Babylon, about B.C. 602, Palestine revolted, the rising being most probably prompted by the Egyptians. Nebuchadnezzar was at the time engaged in other works, and unable to attend to these affairs until B.C. 598, when he once more swept down upon Palestine, attacking Tyre on the way, and marched into Judah. At this time Jehoiakim, king of Judah, died, and was succeeded by his son Jehoiachin, who was scarcely seated on his father's throne when Nebuchadnezzar deposed him, and raised his uncle, Zedekiah, to the kingdom. Nebuchadnezzar desired a ruler in Judah who should owe his throne to Babylon, and be free from Egyptian influence, and he caused Zedekiah to swear by Jehovah to be faithful to himself. Jehoiachin, the late king, who was a mere youth, together with numerous other captives, he carried with him to Babylon. The new Jewish ruler, Zedekiah, did no better than his late brother, and encouraged by the Egyptians, the kings of Tyre and Zidon, Edom, Moab and Ammon sent embassies to Jerusalem about B.C. 593, to concert plans for making a Palestinian confederacy under the leadership of Egypt to revolt against Babylon. They appear to have taken advantage of a good opportunity, Nebuchadnezzar being engaged on his eastern frontier. The Elamites, once a powerful nation, had been crushed by the Assyrians in the reign of Assur-bani-pal, but after the defeat of the Assyrians by the Medes and Babylonians they had revived, and regained considerable strength. Of the circumstances which brought them into contact with the Babylonians we are ignorant, and we know nothing of the history of the war; the final result of the struggle was, however, to extinguish once more the independence of Elam, the country being now annexed to Babylonia.

Soon after this, Nebuchadnezzar, B.C. 589, moved into Syria, and taking up his head-quarters at Riblah, in the land of Hamath, directed his troops against Palestine. Nebuzaradan,[1] his general, laid siege to Jerusalem, the centre of the revolt, where the Jews within the city were divided into two parties, one for submission to the Chaldeans, the other for resistance. At this time Apries or Hophra was king of Egypt; he had entered with spirit into the Palestinian league, and with his fleet had occupied some parts of the Phœnician coast; on the advance of Nebuchadnezzar he assembled his army, and marched against Jerusalem to endeavour to raise the siege of the city. In this effort he was unsuccessful, though at first the Chaldean

[1] In Assyrian Nabu-zira-iddina "Nebo gave a seed."—S

general alarmed by the advance of the Egyptians, retired from the siege. Whether the latter engaged the army of Pharoah we do not know, but certainly he forced the Egyptians to abandon their enterprise, and leave Jerusalem to its fate. On his return accordingly Nebuzaradan pressed the siege with vigour, and in B.C. 587, Jerusalem fell. The Chaldean army marched in and destroyed the city, burning the Temple, and carrying away its sacred vessels and treasures. Zedekiah attempted to save himself by flight, but was captured, and carried before Nebuchadnezzar, who put his sons to death before his face, and then put out his eyes.

Besides Jerusalem several other cities of Judah were plundered and destroyed, and the people carried into captivity.

The surrounding nations of Palestine which had joined in the revolt were punished in their turn, and in B.C. 586 the Babylonian monarch laid siege to Tyre. Tyre at this time was the central city of Mediterranean commerce, and having possession of a powerful fleet, and a position on the sea coast, it was in an excellent condition for resisting a blockade by land. For thirteen years the army of Nebuchadnezzar sat round its walls, and even when the city was taken

(B.C. 573) the conqueror gained very little to reward his toil.[1]

Meanwhile events were happening elsewhere to call off the attention of the Babylonian monarch.

Nebuchadnezzar had wedded the daughter of the king of Media, and this alliance insured the peace between these two nations. The warlike Median monarch did not interfere with the conquests of his great son-in-law, but he, at the same time, sought an empire outside the circle of the Babylonian conquests. On the east of Media, in Armenia, and the eastern part of Asia Minor, the Median empire was extended, and its western border now touched the dominions of the rising Lydian kingdom. Since the time of Gyges Lydia had enjoyed great prosperity, and its territory now embraced a considerable portion of Asia Minor. A dispute arose between Lydia and Media on account of some fugitives, who fled from the court of Cyaxares, king of Media, and took refuge with Alyattes, king of Lydia. In B.C. 590 war broke out between the two powers in consequence of the Lydians refusing to deliver up the fugitives.

This war is said to have lasted five years, with no

[1] It is by no means clear that Nebuchadnezzar did take Tyre. So judicious a historian as Mr. Grote thinks not.—S.

permanent advantage on either side, when, in B.C. 585, while the Lydians and Medes were engaged in battle there happened an eclipse of the sun, and both armies taking this as an omen, the opportunity was seized by the king of Cilicia and Nebuchadnezzar to press a peace upon the combatants.[1]

Meanwhile affairs in Palestine were still unsettled. The Jews had revolted, and murdered Gedaliah, the governor set over them by Nebuchadnezzar, and then many of the people had sought an asylum in Egypt, hoping there to be beyond the vengeance of the Chaldeans. The tribes around Palestine were also disaffected, and Tyre still held out, the length of the siege giving some hopes to the enemies of Babylonia in this direction. A new Chaldean force was sent into Palestine B.C. 582, Judah being again ravaged, and the last of its captives sent to Babylon. It was probably about this time that Nebuchadnezzar punished the tribes on the borders of the desert east of Palestine, and sent an army which penetrated far into Arabia, and nominally added a considerable part of that difficult country to the Babylonian empire.

It is probable that the command of the Mediter-

[1] According to Mr. Hind, this eclipse would have taken place May 28th, B.C. 584.

ranean, then in the hands of the Tyrian fleet, enabled them to remove the bulk of their wealth before the fall of the city. Within the reach of the Babylonian sovereign there still remained Egypt, which had fomented and encouraged every successive rebellion in Palestine. In B.C. 567 Nebuchadnezzar marched in person into that country, and defeating the army of Hophra, overran Egypt, and plundered it of all its wealth. Hophra fell into his hands, and was deposed, a general named Ahmes or Amasis being acknowledged as king of Egypt in his stead, the new monarch being installed as a vassal of Babylonia.

The conquest of Egypt probably closed the era of the foreign wars of Nebuchadnezzar: these contests had lasted at least thirty-three years, and had extended from the confines of Persia in the east to Libya in the west, and from Cilicia in the north to Arabia in the south. The boundaries of the Babylonian kingdom at this time comprised, so far as we know, Elam or Khuzistan on the east, and parts north of this, including Zimri and the region as far as the Zagros mountains, taking in all the best part of Assyria, and probably all the region south of the Mardin mountains, across to Cilicia, where the boundary touched the Mediterranean. All Syria, as far as the Mediterranean, was included, and Egypt, with part of Libya, on the west. It is uncertain if Cyprus owned the sway of Nebuchadnezzar, and nothing is known of most of the states of Asia Minor. On the south the empire was bordered by the Libyan desert, the cataracts of the Nile, and an uncertain line running through Arabia. The Persian Gulf was under Babylonian control, both shores being subject to Nebuchadnezzar, and a considerable commerce was carried on from it to India.

The rapidity with which this empire had been acquired shows the genius of Nabopolassar and his son Nebuchadnezzar. Only forty years before, Babylonia had been subject to Assyria, and within that space the Babylonians had, in conjunction with the Medes, crushed the power of Assyria, conquered its dependencies, broken the power of the monarchy raised by Psammetichus in Egypt, overrun Arabia, and annexed Elam.

The fame of Nebuchadnezzar rests, however, more on his buildings than his conquests. Short outlines and notes in the Bible, and various ancient authors, are all that remain of the political events of his reign, and it is at present impossible to fill in the details of his various campaigns; but he himself has left us in his inscriptions minute and remarkable accounts of his various architectural works. These show precisely the spirit mentioned in the book of Daniel. All his labour and all his glory, were to make Babylon the grandest city of the world; nothing was spared that absolute power could dictate and that wealth or genius could supply, and under Nebuchadnezzar Babylon became the glory and wonder of the world.

The great temple of Babylon, called Saggal, which was dedicated to Merodach or Bel,[1] he rebuilt and richly adorned with gold, silver, and precious stones; and here he once more reared the head of the ziggurrat or tower called Temin-sami-irtsiti, "the foundation of heaven (and) earth." The sanctuary of Bel he roofed with cedar brought from the mountains of Lebanon, and overlaid with gold; the temples of Birbir and Ziru, dedicated to Bel and Rubat, the temple of the Moon god, the temple of the Sun, the temple of Vul, the atmospheric god, the temple of the goddess Gula, the temple of Venus, and other buildings, he reconstructed

[1] Bel-Merodach was termed the younger Bel, to distinguish him from the elder Bel, one of the members of the trinity, Anu, Bel, and Hea. The older Bel was called Mul or Mul-ge, "the lord of the abyss" in Accadian, and presided over the earth and underground world. Bel, Assyrian Bilu, is the Hebrew Baal, "lord."—S.

and beautified. He raised the celebrated hanging gardens, which consisted of arched terraces covered with earth, in which grew all manner of trees and flowers. He rebuilt the great walls of Babylon called Imgur-Bel and Nimit-Bel, and he completed the magnificent palace partly built by his father.

In Borsippa, which lay to the west of Babylon, on the other side of the Euphrates, he rebuilt the temple of Nebo and some smaller shrines. Here was a celebrated temple, probably standing on the site of the traditional tower of Babel. This temple was raised in the form of a truncated pyramid or ziggurrat, but only 42 cubits (70 feet) had been built, and the structure being left unfinished had fallen into ruin. Nebuchadnezzar rebuilt it in the form of a temple of seven stages, each stage being dedicated to one of the planetary bodies.

At all the various cities of Babylonia he rebuilt the principal temples, but nowhere did he lavish such magnificence as at Babylon. Looking down on this proud city, which he had made the mistress of the world, we can well conceive the monarch saying, "Is not this great Babylon that I have built for the house of the kingdom, by the might of my power, and for the honour of my majesty?"

In the court, and among the upper classes, there was at this time a luxury equal to the magnificence of the buildings. Lebanon furnished its cedars, Tyre its goods and manufactures, Helbon, the Shuite district, the north of Assyria and Syria, furnished various wines, which flowed on the royal and priestly tables like rivers; cattle, animals of all sorts, strange birds, and fish, some presents from distant lands, others the plunder of conquered and oppressed nations, filled the fields and waters of Babylon; and the noblest youths of conquered peoples served in the presence of the king and courtiers.

The last ten years of the reign of Nebuchadnezzar appear to have been spent in peace, surrounded by all this pomp and luxury. During this period, according to the book of Daniel, the king suffered for a time under a form of madness, conceiving himself to be a beast of the field. No inscription or notice in confirmation of this has yet been discovered; but it must be remembered that our knowledge of the whole of the reign is very scanty.

So far as we can trace the character of Nebuchadnezzar, he appears to have been a sovereign of great ability, a good general, bold in design, and resolute in action. The long wars he waged over most of the then known world, his defeat of the Egyptians at Carchemish at the outset of his career, and his long and determined blockade of Tyre, show his military character; but, like most Oriental sovereigns, his acts were stained with cruelty. As a builder, Nebuchadnezzar stands in the first rank, and he was a great patron of arts and sciences. His system of government was the usual Eastern one of draining and oppressing conquered countries and subject provinces to increase the glory and magnificence of his capital. In religion Nebuchadnezzar was, like most rulers, faithful to the orthodoxy of his day. Merodach or Bel and Nebo were his great divinities, and after them came a train of lesser gods, who each shared the devotion and gifts of the sovereign. His gods are said to inspire his heart; he acknowledges that his life and success were from them, and he raises at their holy seats prayer and thanksgiving to them.

Such was Nebuchadnezzar, the greatest of the Babylonian sovereigns. He reigned over Western Asia from his campaign against Carchemish, in B.C. 605, until his death, B.C. 562. On the death of Nebuchadnezzar his crown descended to his son Amil-Maruduk, the Evil-Merodach of the Bible, called by the Greeks Ilouarodam.

Evil-Merodach appears, so far as we can judge, to have been a pacific sovereign; but the ancient authors who mention him condemn his government. Nebuchadnezzar had taken captive Jehoiachin, king of Judah, and kept him in prison at Babylon. Evil-Merodach, however, released the captive when he came to the throne, and seated him in honour at Babylon. It is probable that in other respects Evil-Merodach reversed the policy of his father, and this led to discontent among the proud overbearing nobles of Babylon. In consequence of this a conspiracy was formed against him, led by his own brother-in-law Nergal-sar-uzur, the Nergalsharezer of the Bible, called Neri-glissor by the Greek writers, and Evil-Merodach was assassinated after a reign of two years, B.C. 560.

On the murder of Evil-Merodach the conspirators raised to the throne Nergalsharezer, their leader. He was the son of Bel-zakir-iskun, who had ruled at Babylon during the troublous period towards the close of the Assyrian monarchy. It is unknown whether he was the same as the Bel-zakir-iskun who ruled in Assyria about the same time. Nergalsharezer had been appointed *rubu emga* (the Rabmag of the Bible), which appears to have been one of the highest titles in the state, and he received in marriage a daughter of Nebuchadnezzar; thus becoming closely connected with the throne.

He accompanied the Babylonian army to Jerusalem, and is mentioned as sitting in the gate after the taking of the city. At the time of his accession to the throne he was advanced in years, and he only reigned a little more than three years, dying in B.C. 556. Nergalsharezer is only known to have repaired the river front of the Babylonian palace, and to have built a new palace for himself there. Like his predecessor, he engaged in no warlike expeditions, and the military strength of the Babylonian empire slowly declined.

CHAPTER X.

THE DECLINE AND FALL OF THE BABYLONIAN EMPIRE.

Laborosoarchod—Nabonidos—Astyages and Cyrus—Inscriptions of Cyrus—Conquest of Babylon—Return of the Jews from exile—Kambyses and Smerdis—Darius Hystaspes—Revolt and capture of Babylon—Second revolt of Babylon under Arahu —Babylon taken—Decline of Babylon.

THE son and successor of Nergalsharezer was called by the Greeks Laborosoarchod, perhaps a corruption of the Babylonian name Ulbar-surki-idina. This prince had only reigned nine months when a new conspiracy was formed, and he was assassinated; a man named Nabu-imtuk, or Nabu-nahid, called by the Greeks Labynetos or Nabonidos, son of the *rubu emga* or rabmag Nabu-balatsu-iqbi, being raised to the throne B.C. 556. Nabonidos either was a descendant of Nebuchadnezzar on the female side, or married into the family to strengthen his right to the throne. In connection with him we find mentioned in Herodotus a queen named Nitocris, to whom some of the great works at Babylon are ascribed.

Nabonidos reigned for seventeen years and witnessed the rise of a new power in the east. This was the empire of Cyrus, about which the cuneiform records have lately revealed to us information of a startling kind.

Among the tablets found by Mr. Rassam during his excavations in Babylonia are three documents which relate to the reign and overthrow of the last Babylonian king. One of these is a cylinder inscribed by order of Cyrus which describes his greatness and conquests, more especially that of Babylon. The second is an annalistic tablet recounting the events which marked the several years of the reign of Nabonidos, and narrating the history of his overthrow. This also was compiled for Cyrus. The third is a cylinder belonging to Nabonidos, in which he gives an account of his restoration of the temple of the Moon-god at Haran, and of the temples of Anunit and Samas at Sippara. The famous city of Haran, we are told in the last record, had been taken and destroyed by the *Manda* or "barbarians" of Ecbatana, and the temple of the Moon-god had shared the fate of the city. "Then," says Nabonidos, "at the beginning of my long reign,

Merodach, the great lord, and Sin (the Moon-god), the illuminator of heaven and earth, the strong one of the universe, revealed unto me a dream. Merodach spake with me (thus): 'O Nabonidos, king of Babylon, go up with the horse of thy chariot; make bricks for the Temple of Rejoicing, and let the seat of Sin, the great lord, enter within it.' Reverently I spake to Merodach, the lord of the gods: 'I will build this temple whereof thou hast spoken. The barbarians went about it, and their forces were terrible.' Merodach answered me: 'The barbarians of whom thou hast spoken shall not exist, neither they nor their lands, nor the kings their allies.' In the third year when it came when they (*i.e.*, the barbarians) had caused Cyrus, the king of Elam, his young servant, to march amongst his army, they provoked him (to battle); the wide-spread barbarians he overthrew; he captured Astyages, king of the barbarians, and seized his treasures; to his own land he took (them)." After this Nabonidos carried out the will of the gods. His "vast army" was summoned from Gaza on the one side to the Persian Gulf on the other, and employed in restoring the temple of Haran, which had been built three centuries previously by the Assyrian king Shalmaneser II., and subsequently restored by Assur-bani-pal.

The annalistic tablet, which is unfortunately

mutilated, begins with the first year of Nabonidos. The first three years after his accession seem to have been occupied with disturbances in Syria. Then, in the sixth year, "Astyages gathered (his army) and marched against Cyrus, king of Elam. But the soldiers of Astyages revolted from him, and seized him, and delivered him up to Cyrus. Cyrus (proceeded) to the land of Ecbatana, the royal city. The silver, the gold, the furniture, and the spoil of the land of Ecbatana he carried away, and brought the furniture and the spoil which he had taken to the land of Elam.—The seventh year the king (Nabonidos) was in the town of Tema [a suburb of Babylon]. The king's son, the nobles, and his soldiers were in Accad [*i.e.*, northern Babylonia]. The king did not go to Babylon, neither did Nebo nor Bel. But they kept a festival; they sacrificed peace-offerings in the temples of Saggil and Zida to the gods for (the preservation) of Babylon and Borsippa. The governor inspected the garden and the temple.—In the eighth year (no event took place).—The ninth year Nabonidos, the king, was in Tema, the king's son, the nobles, and his soldiers were in Accad. Until the month of Nisan (March) the king did not go to Babylon, neither did Nebo nor Bel. But they kept a festival; they sacrificed peace-offerings to the gods in the temples of Saggil and Zida for the preservation of Babylon and Borsippa. On the 5th day of Nisan, the king's mother, who was in the fortress of the camp on the river Euphrates, above Sippara, died. The king's son and his soldiers mourned for her three days running. In the month Sivan (May) there was a mourning for the king's mother throughout the land of Accad. In the month of Nisan, Cyrus, king of Persia, collected his soldiers and crossed the Tigris below Arbela, and the following month marched against the land of . . . its king took (his) silver and himself; he made his own children mount (the pyre); afterwards both king and children were (burnt) in the midst (of it).—The tenth year the king was in Tema; the king's son, the officers, and his soldiers were in Accad. Until (Nisan) the king (did not go to Babylon), neither did Nebo nor Bel. But they kept the festival; they sacrificed peace-offerings to the gods in the temples (of Saggil and Zida) for the preservation of Babylon and Borsippa. On the 21st day of Sivan (the soldiers) of Elam marched into Accad. A prefect (was appointed?) in Erech.—The eleventh year the king was in Tema; the king's son, the nobles, and the soldiers were in Accad. Until Elul (August) the king did not come forth (to worship) Bel, but they kept the festival;

they sacrificed peace-offerings (to the gods in the temples of Saggil and Zida for the preservation of) Babylon and Borsippa."

Here a break occurs in the record. When the inscription again becomes legible the events of the seventeenth and last year of Nabonidos are being recounted. The tribes on the Persian Gulf were now in revolt. Cyrus, who had failed to break through the Babylonian army in Accad, had spent his time in intriguing with a disaffected party, who were probably the Jews, in the heart of Babylonia itself, and as soon as all was ready prepared to attack Nabonidos from the south-east. The king of Babylon turned to the gods in his extremity and caused their images to be brought to the capital city, in the hope that their presence would protect it from attack. "The gods of Marad, Zamama and the gods of Kis, Beltis and the gods of Kharsak-kalama, were brought to Babylon; up to the end of Elul, the gods of Accad which are above and below the sky were being brought to Babylon; but the gods of Borsippa, Cuthah, and Sippara were not brought. In the month Tammuz (June) Cyrus gave battle to the army of Accad in the town of Rutum upon the river Nizallat. The men of Accad broke into revolt. The men were slain. On the 14th day Sippara was taken without fighting. Nabonidos flies. On the 16th day Gobryas, the governor of Gutium (Kurdistan), and the army of Cyrus entered Babylon without fighting. Afterwards he takes Nabonidos, and puts him into fetters at Babylon. Up to the end of the month Tammuz some rebels from Kurdistan kept the gates of the temple of Saggil closed, but there was nothing in the way of weapons in the temple of Saggil, nor was there an opportunity (for fighting). On the 3rd day of Marchesvan (October) Cyrus entered Babylon. The roads before him were covered. He grants peace to the city, to the whole of Babylon Cyrus proclaims peace. Gobryas, his governor, was appointed over the (other) governors in Babylon, and from the month Chisleu (November) to the month Adar (February) the gods of Accad, whom Nabonidos had brought to Babylon, were restored to their shrines. On the 11th day of the previous Marchesvan, Gobryas (was appointed) over Babylon, and the king (Nabonidos) died. From the 27th of Adar to the 3rd of Nisan (there was) a mourning in Accad; all the people smote their heads. On the 4th day Kambyses, the son of Cyrus, arranged the burial in the Temple of the Sceptre of the World. The priests of the Temple of the Sceptre of Nebo went (to it)." The text after this is too much broken for a connected translation. It describes the honours paid by Cyrus and his son to the Babylonian deities, the sacrifices they made to Bel, and their restoration of Nebo to his old shrine.

The history is completed by the cylinder-inscription of Cyrus, which states that the gods had been offended with Nabonidos in consequence of his neglect of them. "The gods dwelling within them left their shrines in anger when (Nabonidos) brought them into Babylon. Merodach went about to all men wherever were their seats; and the men of Sumer and Accad, whom he had sworn should attend him (besought him to return). The favour he granted; he came back; all lands, even the whole of them, rejoiced and ate. And he appointed a king to guide aright in the heart what his hand upholds; Cyrus, king of Elam, he proclaimed by name for the sovereignty; all men everywhere commemorate his name. The men of Gutium (Kurdistan) and all the barbarians (*Manda*) [of Ecbatana] he made bow down to his feet, the men of the blackheaded race [*i.e.*, the Accadians], whom he had conquered with his hands, he governed in justice and righteousness. Merodach, the great lord, the restorer of his people, beheld with joy the deeds of his vicegerent, who was righteous in hand and heart.

To his city of Babylon he summoned his march, and he bade him take the road to Babylon; like a friend and a comrade he went at his side. The weapons of his vast army, whose number, like the waters of a river, could not be known, he marshalled at his side. Without fighting or battle he caused him to enter into Babylon; his city of Babylon feared; in a place difficult of access Nabonidos, the king, who worshipped him not, he gave into his hand. The men of Babylon, all of them, (and) the whole of Sumer and Accad, the nobles and priests who had revolted, kissed his feet; they rejoiced in his sovereignty; their faces shone. The god who in his ministry raises the dead to life, who benefits all men in difficulty and prayer, has in goodness drawn nigh to him, has made strong his name. I am Cyrus, the king of multitudes, the great king, the powerful king, the king of Babylon, the king of Sumer and Accad, the king of the four zones, the son of Kambyses the great king, the king of Elam; the grandson of Cyrus the great king, the king of Elam; the great-grandson of Teispes the great king, the king of Elam; of the ancient seed-royal, whose rule has been beloved by Bel and Nebo, whose sovereignty they cherished according to the goodness of their hearts. At that time I entered

Babylon in peace. With joy and gladness in the palace of the kings I enlarged the seat of my dominion. Merodach, the great lord, (cheered) the heart of his servant, whom the sons of Babylon (obeyed each) year and day. . . . My vast armies he marshalled peacefully in the midst of Babylon; throughout Sumer and Accad I had no revilers. The sanctuaries of Babylon and all its fortresses I established in peace. As for the sons of Babylon . . . their ruins I repaired, and I delivered their prisoners. For the work (of restoring the shrine) of Merodach, the great lord, I prepared, and he graciously drew nigh unto me, Cyrus, the king, his worshipper, and to Kambyses, my son, the offspring of my heart, and to all my army, and in peace we duly restored its front (in) glory. All the kings who dwell in the highplaces of all regions from the Upper Sea to the Lower Sea, who dwell in (the highplaces) of the kings of Phœnicia and Sutar, all of them brought their rich tribute, and in the midst of Babylon kissed my feet. From (the city of) . . . to the cities of Assur and Istar . . . Accad, Marad, Zamban, Me-Turnat, and Duran as far as the border of Kurdistan, the fortresses (which lie) upon the Tigris, wherein from of old were their seats, I restored the gods who dwell within them to their places, and I enlarged (for them) seats that should be long-enduring; all their peoples I assembled, and I restored their lands. And the gods of Sumer and Accad, whom Nabonidos, to the anger of the lord of gods (Merodach), had brought into Babylon, I settled in peace in their sanctuaries by the command of Merodach, the great lord. In the goodness of their hearts may all the gods whom I have brought into their strong places daily intercede before Bel and Nebo that they should grant me length of days; may they bless my projects with prosperity, and may they say to Merodach, my lord, that Cyrus, the king, thy worshipper, and Kambyses, his son (deserve thy favour)."

These inscriptions oblige us to reconstruct the history of Cyrus and the rise of the Persian Empire which we have received from the classical writers. It appears that Cyrus and his predecessors were not kings of Persia but of Anzan or Elam, and that he did not obtain possession of Persia till after his conquest of Astyages between the sixth and ninth years of Nabonidos (B.C. 549–546). Darius Hystaspes and not Cyrus was the real founder of the Persian Empire, and we can now understand why it is that in Isaiah xxi. 2 the forces of Elam and Media are called upon to overthrow Babylon. It further appears that the subjects of Istuvegu or Astyages were not really the Medes—a name first given by the Assyrians to the tribes who lived eastward of Kurdistan,—but a people who were called *manda* or "barbarians" by the Babylonians, and that this word *manda* has been confounded with *Mada* or "Medes" by the Persians and Greeks. The word *manda* was used as early as the time of Sargon I. of Agadé, since it occurs in the great astronomical work which was compiled for his library, and it is also applied by Esarhaddon to Teuspa the Kimmerian.

Perhaps the most startling fact recorded in the inscriptions is that Babylon surrendered to Gobryas the general of Cyrus without a siege. The siege, therefore, described by Herodotus, must have been one of those undergone by the city during the reign of Darius, which has been falsely transferred to the age of Cyrus. Equally false is the description of the line of march which according to the Greek historian was followed by Cyrus. Cyrus entered Babylonia from the south-east (as is stated in Isaiah xxi. 2), and not from the north; the army of Nabonidos stationed near Sippara had prevented him from forcing an entrance into the country on this side. While, therefore, he remained on the northern frontier of Babylonia he had to content himself with completing his conquest of the outlying portions of the empire of Astyages. The city whose king burnt himself with his treasures and children lest he might fall into the hands of the enemy may have been either Larissa or Mespila (Muspilu), two towns described by Xenophon as situated near the ruins of Nineveh and destroyed by Cyrus. At all events, Cyrus had to pass Arbela, the city of Istar, before reaching it, and on his cylinder he claims to have captured the cities of Assur and Istar, Assur being the modern Kalah Sherghat, the primitive capital of Assyria, while "the city of Istar" was Arbela.

The queen-mother, whose death in the camp at Sippara was regarded as an event of so much consequence, may have been the Nitokris of the Greek writers. The fortifications built to resist the invasion of Cyrus were assigned to her, and the fact that she died in the camp seems to show that she possessed a military spirit which was wanting in Nabonidos. The "king's son" who was in command of the army was doubtless Bilu-sarra-utsur or Belshazzar. Nabonidos mentions him by name as his eldest son in one of his inscriptions.

In harmony with what we read in the Bible, the cylinder of Cyrus tells us that the first occupation of the conqueror was to restore the exiles who had been transported into Babylonia by former Chaldean kings. His own experience had taught him how dangerous it was to have a disaffected population in the heart of the country. But the restoration of the Jewish captives could have had nothing to do with his own religious faith, as has sometimes been supposed, partly because the Jews were not the only people allowed to return to their homes, partly because the language of Cyrus shows plainly that he was a polytheist. The idea, therefore, so long maintained, that he was a Zoroastrian monotheist must be abandoned. The Persians, and not the Elamites, were Zoroastrians, and though Cyrus was by descent a Persian, as is shown by the name of his great-grandfather Teispes, he was by birth and education an Elamite. The theory, consequently, that the doctrine of the resurrection was learnt by the Jewish exiles from the Persians can never again be advanced.

Two years before his death Cyrus made his son Kambyses "king of Babylon," reserving to himself the imperial title of "king of the world." He died B.C. 529, leaving his crown to Kambyses, under whom there was little change in the condition of Babylonia. The people, however, were dissatisfied with the foreign dominion, and secretly prepared to revolt against Persia, only waiting for an opportunity to throw off the yoke of their conquerors.

An opportunity soon occurred: Kambyses was absent in Egypt (which he conquered B.C. 527) during the latter part of his reign, and some dissatisfaction arose in Media and Persia in consequence. The dissatisfaction among the Medes was increased by the feeling that whereas Media had been the chief state, it was now subject to Persia, which had once been tributary to it.

Kambyses had secretly murdered his younger brother Bardes, or Smerdis, and this fact appears to have been unknown among the people. A Median, one of the Magi, named Gumatu or Gomates, taking advantage of the disaffection during the absence of Kambyses, personated the dead prince Smerdis, and declaring himself son of Cyrus, rose in rebellion B.C. 522, and Media and Persia went over to him. Kambyses, on hearing of the revolt, left Egypt in haste to meet the pretender, but killed himself (perhaps by accident) in Syria while on the road to Persia. Soon afterwards the Magian usurper was killed by Darius, son of Hystaspes ("Ancient Hist. from the Monuments: Persia," pp. 29, 30, S.P.C.K.), and Darius mounted the throne of Persia.

During these troubles the Babylonians were preparing to revolt, and a man arose among them named Nadintu-Bel, son of Aniri, who declared himself to be Nebuchadnezzar, son of Nabonidus, the late Babylonian sovereign.

Under this man the Babylonians revolted on the accession of Darius, B.C. 522, and at the same time Susiana threw off the yoke of Persia. Darius, after sending a deputy, who conquered the Susians, proceeded himself against Babylon. On arriving at the Tigris, the Persian monarch found the Babylonians had command of the river, and opposed his crossing; they had removed the ferry-boats, and posted their forces opposite the road, but Darius passed his troops over the river, and defeated the Babylonian army; after which he marched towards Babylon, and reached the Euphrates at the town of Zazan, near Babylon, where the pretended Nebuchadnezzar again offered battle. In the second engagement the Persians were again triumphant, the Babylonians being routed, and part of their forces driven into the river. Nadintu-Bel fled with a few of his soldiers, and took refuge in Babylon, where he was followed and captured by Darius, who executed him for his rebellion about B.C. 521.

For some years after this Babylon remained subject to Persia, but about B.C. 515 a man named Arahu, son of Handita, arose at a town named Duban, and, like Nadintu-Bel, personated Nebuchadnezzar, son of Nabonidus. The people of Babylon again revolted, and making this man king, prepared to resist Darius. The Persian monarch sent a general, who advanced to Babylon, and besieged Arahu there. How long the siege lasted we are not told, but the Persians captured the city, and taking Arahu prisoner, crucified him.

With the crushing of the second revolt against Persia ends the monumental history of Babylonia; its history after this is only the history of a province of the successive empires of the East. It is true that the Babylonian religion survived, and the cuneiform writing continued to be used for some centuries; but these also in time perished, and at the time of the Christian era everything but the Babylonian superstitions and astrology had passed away.

After the Persian conquest Babylon remained one of the capitals of the empire, and it retained this position until the rise of the city of Seleucia, after which Babylon gradually decayed, until its palaces became mounds of rubbish, in which it is impossible to recognize the outlines and features of the original buildings.

The fall of Babylon was brought about through the vice and corruption of the religion and morals of the country. The numerous deities, the slavish superstitions, the obscene rites of the goddesses, the debasing ignorance of the bulk of the people, and the indolence begotten of triumph and pillage, combined with a general moral and mental decay, were more disastrous to the country than the arms of the Persian conquerors.

EXPLANATION OF BABYLONIAN PROPER NAMES.

[*Added by the Editor.*]

THE derivation of Babylonian proper names has to be sought in four different languages. The oldest names belong to the agglutinative Accadian, the later to the inflectional Semitic. Besides these, there are other proper names, the explanation of which is to be found in the allied dialects of Elam and the Cassi (Kossæans), which belong to the same family of speech as the Accadian.

ACCADIAN NAMES.

Ubara-Tutu, Servant of the setting sun.
Merodach, The brilliance of the sun.
Hea, The god of the house.
Dav-kina, The mistress of the earth.
Na (*or Anu*), The sky.
Nana, Lady.
Dumuzi (*Tammus*), The offspring, or only son.
Siduri, The eye of youth.
Lig-Bagas, A lion (is) the goddess Bagas.
Dungi, The powerful.
Ri-Agu (*or Eri-Aku, or Rim-Agu*), The servant of the moon-god.
Agu-kak-rimi, The moon-god (is) the maker of our light.
Sipar (*Sippara*), The shrine of the sun.
Accad (*Acada*), The highlands.
Ur (*or Muru, or Eri*), The city.
Erech (*Uruki*), The city of the land.
E-Saggal, House of the high head.
Silim-kalama, Couch of the world.

ELAMITE NAMES.

Kudur-Mabuk, Servant of Mabuk.
Kudur-Nanhundi. Servant of Nankhunta.
Kudur-Lagamar (*Chedorlaomer*), Servant of Lagamar.
Te-umman, Worshipper of Umman.

Cassite Names.

Khammuragas, Extensive family.
Kara-indas, Servant of Indas.
Burna-buriyas, Servant of Buryas.
Nazi-bugas, A prince (is) Bugas (*Bagas*).
Meli-sipak, The man of Sipak.
Gan-duniyas, The enclosure of Duniyas.

Semitic Names.

Busur-sadi-rabi, The defence (?) of the great mountain.
Hea-bani, Hea (is) my creator.
Ismi-Dagan, Dagon has heard.
Naram-Sin, The chosen of the moon-god.
Assur-yubalidh, Assur gave life.
Muballidhat-Seruya, The quickened of Seruya.
Bel-nirari, Bel (is) my help.
Shalmaneser (*'Sallimanu-esar*), Shalman guides straight.
Merodach-baladan (*Maruduk-bal-iddina*), Merodach gave a son.
Zamama-zakir-idina, Zamama gave a memorial.
Nebuchadrezzar (*Nabu-kudura-utsur*), Nebo, defend [*or* has created] the crown, *or* landmark.
Assur-ris-ilim, Assur, the head of the gods.
Tiglath-pileser (*Tugulti-pal-esar*), The servant of (the god) the son of Bit-Esar.
Assur-bel-kala, Assur, the lord of all.
Maruduk-sapik-tsirrat, Merodach, the heaper up of dominion.
Hea-mukin-ziri, Hea, establisher of a seed.
Maruduk-nadin-akhi, Merodach, the giver of brethren.
Samsu-iluna, The sun-god (is) our god.
Nabu-zakir-iscun, Nabo established the memorial.
Assur-natsir-pal, Assur, the protector of the son.
Musallimu-Maruduk, Merodach (is) a completer.
Maruduk-baladhsu-ikbi, Merodach announced his life.
Nabu-yusabsi, Nebo caused to exist.
Kin-ziru, Establish a seed.
Sennacherib (*'Sin-akhi-erba*), The moon-god increased brothers.
Bel-ibni, Bel created.
Assur-nadin-sum(*i*), Assur, the giver of a name.
Nabu-zir-napisti-esir, Nebo guides straight the seed of life.
Esarhaddon (*Assur-akhi-iddina*), Assur gave brothers.
Bel-basa,, Bel exists.
Assur-dayan, Assur(is) judge.
Assur-bani-pal, Assur, create a son.

Assur-dur-utsur, Assur, defend the fortress.
Sin-tabni-utsur, Sin, defend the offspring.
Mannu-ki-babili, What (is) like Babylon?
Hea-mubasa, Hea (is) he that makes exist.
Nabopolassar (*Nabu-pal-utsur*), Nebo, protect (*or* has created) the son.
Evil-Merodach (*Amil-Maruduk*), The man of Merodach.
Nergal-šarra-utsur, Nergal, protect (*or* has created) the king.
Ulbar-surki-iddina, The god of Bit-Ulbar gave presents.
Nabonidus (*Nabu-nahid*), Nebo is glorious. (The Accadian equivalent of *nahid* is *imtuk*.)
Nadintu-Bel, The gift of Bel.
Bel (*Bilu*), Lord.
Nabo (*Nabiu*, or *Nabu*), The prophet.
Tasmit, The hearer.
Saru, The wind.
Bab-salimiti, Gate of peace.
Babylon (*Bab-ili*), Gate of God.
Elam (*Elamu*), The Highlands (the Semitic rendering of the native name *Khabarti*, or *Khubur; Numma* in Accadian).
Me-Turnat, The waters of the Tornadotus.
Kar-Assur, Fort of Assur.
Imgur-Bel, The beloved (?) of Bel.
Nimit-Bel (or rather *Nemid-Bel*), The foundation of Bel.

INDEX.

ACCAD, or AKKAD, a district originally named from the city of Agadé, a part of Sippara, n. p. 61; first four cities, Babel, Erech, Akkad, and Calneh, p. 61; the country of classical cuneiform literature, from which all the great Assyrian works were copied, 81.

Accadian language and literature, 18; libraries at Agadé, Senkereh, Ur, Erech, and Cuthah, 19; charms or magic formulæ, divination and omens, dread of the powers of evil, hymn to the seven baleful spirits, 20–22; hymns to the gods compiled B.C. 2000, compared with the Rig-Veda, 23, 24; hymns to Merodach and Samas, 24, 25; penitential psalm, 26, 27; prayer, 27; mythological poems founded on astronomy, 29; hymns translated into Assyrian, 29; laws relating to slaves, legal precedents and decisions, 30, 31; respect for women, 30; language agglutinative, 35, n.

Adrahasis, or Hasisadra, compared with Noah, 37.

Agu-kak-rimi restored the temple of Bel at Babylon, and ransomed the images of Merodach and Zirat-banit from the land of Hani, 83.

Ashdod besieged by the Egyptians, who also wrested Carchemish from the Assyrians, 155, 157.

Amraphel, or Amarpul, 98.

Amil-Maruduk, the Biblical Evil-Merodach, a mild and peaceful ruler; released Jehoiachin, but detained him in honourable captivity; murdered by his brother-in-law, 173, 174.

Antiquity and extent of Babylonian civilization, 14, 32.

Anu, the god of heaven; Anatu, his consort, 57.

Arahu, a Babylonian pretender, crucified by Darius, 191.

Arioch, Eri-aku, or Rim-agu, son of Kudur-mabug, 99, n.

Arts and sciences cultivated by the Babylonians, 15.

Astronomy derived from Chaldæa, 15.

Assur-dayan sent expeditions against Ituha and Gananati, 115.

Assur-nazir-pal defeated the Shuites and Babylonians, and subdued the region of the Khabur, 107, 108.

Assur-ubalid's daughter married to the king of Babylonia, 91.

Athara, the city where the chiefs of Pekod and Hindaru submitted and paid tribute to Sargon, 125.
BABEL, "gate of God," the Semitic rendering of Ca-Dimirra, possibly in reference to the building of the Tower, 53, n.
Bab-salimiti, a city on the Persian Gulf, 13, 14, 137.
Babylon, city of, built in very early times, 81; asserted by the Babylonians to have been a great city before the Deluge, 53; a place of little importance till it became the capital, and held this position more than 1,200 years, 81; first made sole capital by Khammuragas, who greatly enriched it, and added splendour to its worship of Merodach or Bel, 87, 88; captured by Tiglath-pileser, 103; by Shalmaneser, 110; by Sargon, 127, 128; by Sennacherib, 132; by the Elamites and Chaldæans, 137; again by Sennacherib, given up to indiscriminate plunder, completely destroyed, and the great canal filled up with the ruins, 141, 142; rebuilt by Esar-haddon, 145; captured by Assur-bani-pal, when Saul-mugina set fire to his own palace and perished in the flames, 153; the city rose into greater importance under Nabopolassar, and his son, Nebuchadnezzar, became the centre of the political world, 159; the latter restored its walls, temples, and palaces on a scale of great magnificence whilst engaged in wars with the adjoining countries, 160–171; boast, "Is not this great Babylon?" &c., 171; its wealth and luxury, 172, 173; the Persian conquest under Cyrus, 182, 183; the city captured by Darius, who put the pretender, Nadintu-Bel, to death, and again, a few years afterwards, when Arahu, who had personated a son of Nabonidus, was taken prisoner and crucified, 190–191; causes of its fall, 192.
Babylonia, boundaries of, varied at different periods, 34; thought to have been first peopled by Turanians, who were conquered and dispossessed by Semites, 34, 35; history of the country translated by Berosus from its own records into Greek in the third century B.C., now lost except a few fragments, 35.
Babylonian kings, lists of, &c., 8–12.
Babylonian libraries, 19; mathematical works, tables of squares and cubes now in British Museum from Senkereh, 19; literature, including beast-fables, contract tablets, deeds of sale, geographical lists, chronological tables, historical documents, copies of correspondence, catalogues of animals, trees, stones, &c., &c., 31, 32.
Babylonian proper names: Accadian, Elamite, Cassite, and Semitic, 193–5.
Babylonian religion, a mixture of graceful myths and the worship of stocks and stones, 15, 16.

Bel and Nebo, temples of, plundered by the Elamites, 100; by Suzub, 140.
Bel-Merodach, 170, n.
Bel-nirari routed the Kassu, slew Nazi-bugas, and placed a son of Burna-buriyas on the Babylonian throne, 92.
Bel-shazzar, 188.
Bel-zakir-iskun defeated by the Assyrian general, Nabu-pal-uzur, who was rewarded with the crown of Babylonia on his subjugation of the country, 155, 156.
Birs Nimrúd, view of, 82.
Burna-buriyas confirmed a previous treaty respecting the frontiers of Babylonia and Assyria, 91.
CALAH, revolt at, ended in the elevation of Tiglath-pileser, 116.
Chaldæan accounts of creation and fall of man, 51, 52; of Babel, Sippara, Larancha, and Surippak before the Deluge, 53.
Chaldees, origin of, unknown; some of the early dynasties styled Chaldæan; called Caldai on the monuments, and first obtained possession of Babylon, B.C. 722, under Merodach-baladan, 110, 111.
Cherdorlaomer and his confederates ravaged and plundered Palestine, and retired with great booty; surprised in a night attack near Damascus, 98, 99.
Cities of Babylonia, 16, 18.
Comparison of the Chaldæan account of the Deluge with that in the Bible, 48, 51.
Creation, legend from, Cuthah, 19.
Cuneiform writing invented by Turanians, 16; characters at first hieroglyphics, afterwards represented mere sounds, 17.
Cylindrical seals, 32.
Cyrus threw off the Median yoke, overran and annexed various countries; took Sardis, and put an end to the Lydian kingdom; conquered Babylon; permitted the Jews to return and rebuild Jerusalem, and allowed the conquered Babylonians to retain their own worship, 177–88.
DAKKURI, a Chaldæan tribe, 145.
Darius, son of Hystaspes, slew the impostor Gomates, and mounted the Persian throne; vigorously repressed the revolts in Elam and Babylonia, putting to death Nadintu-Bel, the pretended son of Nabonidus; his general captured Arahu, another pretender, and crucified him, 190, 191.
Destruction of Babylon by Sennacherib, 142.
Division of Assyria on the fall of Nineveh, 158–161.
Dungi, a great builder of temples, 76.
Dur, or Diru, 18, 114, 122.
Duran, or Duban, 18, 138.
Dur-athara taken by Sargon; rebuilt, and its name changed to Dur-Nabu, 125.

Dur-kuri-galzu (Akkerkuf), built by Kur-galzu, 93; seized by Tiglath-pileser, 102.
Dur-papsukul captured by Sargon, 112, 113.
Dur-sar, an Elamite fortress, taken from Samsi-Rimmon, 128.
Dur-yakin, the first seat of Merodach-baladan's government, 124, 129, 130.
EDEN identified with Gan-duniyas, 52, 63.
Elam, peopled by warlike Turanians, often ruled by several petty princes; chief cities, Shushan, Madaktu, and Hidalu, 97.
Eleventh deluge tablet throws light on Genesis account, 38.
Esar-haddon rebuilt Babylon, restored the images of the gods, 145; checked the Dakkuri, burnt their king Samas-ibni, and received Bel-basa's submission; released Manasseh, &c., 146–8.
Evil-Merodach. (See AMIL-MARUDUK.)
Etanna, the mythical founder of Babel, Tammuz, and Ner, 62.
FALL of Assyria, the era of a purer faith, 159.
Fast of 100 days at Nineveh, 156, n.
Frontiers of Assyria definitely settled by treaty, 109, 110.
GAN-DUNI, or KAR-DUNIAS, identified with Eden, by Sir H. C. Rawlinson, 52, 53.
Gudea of Sirgulla, 64.
HAMMURABI, or KHAMMURAGAS, the Cassite conqueror of Babylonia, and founder of a new dynasty; made Babylon sole capital, and added splendour to the worship of Merodach or Bel; was a builder of temples, palaces, and founded several cities, besides excavating the canal named in his honour, Hammu-rabinuhus-nisi, 87–9.
Harbi-Sipak, or Murgas-Sipak, 90.
Harris-kalama, or Kharsak-kalama, 82, 132.
Hea-bani, the astrologer, and friend of Izdubar, 58.
Hea-mubasa, a Chaldæan chief, 151.
Hea-mukin-ziru, a Chaldæan usurper, 104.
ILULÆUS, or YUGÆUS, king of Babylon, 120.
Inda-bigas, king of Elam, 153, 154.
Iriba-Maruduk, name of a king, only found on a weight, 106.
Ishtar, the celebrated queen of Erech, 55; offers to marry Izdubar, and her revenge on his refusal, 55–7.
Ishtar, the goddess, the Biblical Ashtoreth, 55, n.
Ismi-dagan, and Libit-Ishtar, kings of Karrak, 77.
Izdubar, supposed to be Nimrod, made Erech his capital; friendship with Hea-bani, exploits and mythical adventures, 54–7; journey to Hasisadra, who relates to him the story of the Flood, 58, 59.
KAMBYSES murdered his brother Smerdis, conquered Egypt, but was harassed in the latter part of his reign by revolts, and accidentally killed whilst hastening to Persia to put down Gomates, 189, 190.

Kara-hardas, or Kara-Murdas, son of a daughter of Assur-ubalid, 91, 92.
Kara-indas, titles assumed by him, and his treaty with Assur-bel-nisi-su, 90, 91.
Kara-samas, a city on the Tigris, founded by Hammurabi, 89.
Karrak, fall of, used as an era, 80.
Kassu, tribe of, first mentioned in an inscription of Aga-kak-rimi, murdered the king of Babylon, and set up Nazi-bugas, 92.
Kassu-nadin-ahi, the successor of Hea-mukin-ziru, 104.
Kisu (Hymer), a city where Hammurabi restored the temple of Zamama, and built a famous tower, 88.
Kudur-lagamar (see CHEDORLAOMER), 98.
Kudur-nanhundi invaded Babylonia, and carried away the image of Nana, 97, 98.
Kuri-galzu restored several Chaldæan temples, and founded a strong city near Baghdad, 93.
LARSA (Senkereh) became the capital of Riagu's dominions after the fall of Karrak, 77, 80.
MANNU-KA-BILI, a chief of the Dakkuri, 151.
Maruduk-baladsu-iqbi vanquished by Samsi-Rimmon, who captured his whole camp, the royal chariots, pavilion, and couch, 111–13.
Maruduk-zakir-izkur, assisted by the Assyrians, quelled a rebellion headed by his own brother, who was slain after his flight to Halman, 109, 110.
Merodach-baladan I., the successor of Mili-Sipak, routed by Rimmon-nirari, whoravaged Upper Babylonia, and wrested from him the regionof the Khabur, 93.
Merodach-baladan II. rebuilt the temple of Erech, 106.
Merodach-baladan, the contemporary of Sargon and Sennacherib, struggled bravely for nearly thirty years to maintain the independence of Babylonia; formed alliances with the Elamites, and sent an embassy to Hezekiah; was twice defeated and captured, and sent prisoner to Nineveh, but again escaped; murdered Hagisa or Akises, and mounted the Babylonian throne, 121–131; this defection brought Sennacherib against him, who, after the disastrous battle at Kisu, entered Babylon in triumph, plundered the palace, and destroyed nearly all the neighbouring cities and villages, and appointed Bel-ibni as governor; left a force to watch for Merodach-baladan, and returned to Assyria, 132, 133; in despair the fugitive king collected his adherents and the images of his gods, sailed down the Persian Gulf, and founded a Chaldæan colony in Elam, where he died, 132.
Merodach-nadin-ahi worsted Tugulti-pal-esar, and carried away the images of Rimmon and Sala from Hekali, but was

himself completely overthrown the next year, when the Assyrians seized Babylon, and nearly all the important cities, 102, 103.

Merodach-sapik-zirrat made peace with Assur-bel-kala, 103.

Merodach's war with Tiamat compared with that of Michael and the great dragon, 52, 53, n.

Media, rise of, under Cyaxares, 155.

Medo-Persians excelled the older empires in government and military discipline, 159.

Mili-Sipak, son of Kuri-galzu; father of Merodach-baladan I., 93.

NABU-IMTUK, or NABU-NAHID, ascended the throne after the assassination of Laborosoarchod, 176; conquered by Cyrus, 181–2.

Nabu-kudur-uzur (Nebuchadnezzar), the son of Nabu-pal-uzur, made Babylonia the mistress of the surrounding countries, 159–60; surprised and routed the Egyptians at Carchemish, and pushed his way, almost unopposed, to the frontiers of Egypt, 162; received the submission of Jehoiachim, and a few years later deposed Jehoiachin, and set up his uncle, Zedekiah, in his stead, as king of Judah, 163; crushed the power of Elam, and returned to Syria, fixed his head-quarters at Riblah, besieged Tyre, and sent his general, Nebuzaradan against Jerusalem, who captured the king whilst attempting to escape, plundered the city, burnt and razed it to the ground, besides carrying away most of the inhabitants as prisoners, 163–166; left Gedaliah as governor, who was murdered by some disaffected Jews, and the country was again ravaged and depopulated as a punishment, 167; he then went forward, overran and plundered Egypt, deposed Hophra, and set up Ahmes as a vassal king, 168; his conquests, 168, 169; more famous as a builder than a conqueror, rebuilt and adorned all the great temples, but lavished his wealth most on Babylon, making it the grandest city in the world, 168–72; the chief and lesser divinities shared alike his devotion and gifts, 173.

Nabu-pal-idina joined the Shuites against the Assyrians, but sustained a terrible reverse (see ASSUR-NAZIR-PAL), 107.

Nabu-pal-uzur rapidly improved the defences of Babylonia, and began the career of conquest so ably carried on by his illustrious son, Nebuchadnezzar, 159–62.

Nabu-zakir-iskun was unable to repel the Assyrian invaders, who wrested from him several cities on the Tigris, including Baghdad, or rather Khudadu, 106, 107.

Nabu-zir-napisti-esir seized his father's original dominions, and tried to recover all Babylonia, but was beaten by the Assyrians, and fled to Elam, where he was murdered, 144.

Nedintu-Bel, the pretended son of Nebuchadnezzar, put to death by Darius, 190, 191.

Nahid-Maruduk, on submitting to Esar-haddon, appointed governor of his brother's forfeited territory, 145.
Naram-Sin, completed Bit-Ulbar, 86.
Nazi-bugas, a usurper, defeated and slain by Bel-nirari, who placed a son of Burna-buriyas on the throne, 92.
Nazi-murudas, beaten by the Assyrians at Kar-istar-agarsal, 93, 94.
Nebuchadnezzar. (See NABU-KUDUR-UZUR.)
Nergal-sharezer assumed the crown after the murder of Evil-Merodach; was present at the taking of Jerusalem; built a new palace, and restored an old structure, 174, 175.
Ningal-idina, the Assyrian governor of Ur, besieged by Nabu-zir-napisti-esir, 144.
Nipur (Niffer), the parent city of Ur, devoted to the worship of Bel, Belat, and Ninip, 69, 70; no records of its primeval history; walls restored by Rimmon-pal-idina, 106.
OANNES, a fabulous being, said to have taught the arts of civilized life to the Babylonians, 36.
PORUS, or PUL, thought to be Tiglath-pileser, 120.
REVOLT against Assur-bani-pal by Chaldæa, Arabia, Syria, Lydia, Palestine, Egypt, and Elam, 148–51; the confederate armies expelled the Assyrian garrisons from Babylonia, and fortified Sippara, Babylon, Borsippa, and Cutha, as military centres, which were successively taken by the Assyrians, 151, 152.
Rim-agu, or Ri-agu, during a peace of thirty years, largely developed the internal resources and wealth of his country till it was attacked and conquered by Hammurabi, 80.
Rimmon-nirari III., engaged several years in wars with Syria, Media, Dur, and Ituha, 114.
Rimmon-pal-idina restored the walls of Nipur, and rebuilt the temple at Kisu, 106.
Rimmon-zakir-uzur had some disputes with his Assyrian contemporaries, 106.
SAGA-SALTIYAS restored the temples at the two Sipparas, 90.
Sammuramat, wife of Rimmon-nirari, 115.
Samsi-Rimmon utterly routed the Babylonians and their mercenaries at Ahadaba, seized many of the important towns, and burnt hundreds of villages (see Merodach-baladsu-iqbi), 111–13; renewed the war soon after, took Dur, and celebrated a festival to its great god, 113.
Samsu-iluna, the successor of Hammurabi, excavated a large canal named after himself, repaired Dur-Sargina, and made images overlaid with gold for the temples of Saggal, Parra, and Larsa, 89.
Saparda, the Biblical Sepharad, 157, n.
Sargon the Babylonian Moses, his birth, exposure, and adoption, by Akki; conquered the Elamites, Syrians, and Kazalla, 84,

85; besieged in his own capital, successful sally and rout of the rebels, ravaged Subarti with fire and sword, 85, 86; a great builder of temples and palaces, and founder of the city Dur-Sargina, left nearly all the surrounding countries tributary to his successor, 86.

Sargon II., soon after his accession crushed the revolt in Palestine, and then marched against Merodach-baladan and his Elamite allies, drove the latter into their own territory, and wasted a part of Babylonia, 122, 123; engaged in wars the next ten years with Syria, Media, and Armenia, 122, 123; Merodach-baladan ruled well, and prepared for the renewal of hostilities, and fortified Dur-athara to stop Sargon's advance; but the city was captured with immense booty and prisoners; fourteen of the principal cities by the river Ukni were taken and plundered, and two Elamite forts, and Suturnanhundi compelled to retreat with his army to his mountain territories, 123–25; next advanced towards Babylon, and Merodach-baladan retreated to Iqbi-Bel, 126; he entered Babylon in triumph, and offered costly sacrifices to the gods 126, 127; Merodach-baladan next retired with all his forces to Dur-yakin, where he was defeated with great slaughter, and all his treasures captured; he then submitted to Sargon, and was carried into captivity with his wife and children, 128; the conqueror secured the friendship of the priesthood by restoring the rites and offerings of the various gods, and reigned at Babylon five years, where he received two embassies from distant countries, 128, 129.

Sennacherib, on ascending the throne, resided at Nineveh, and appointed his brother governor of Babylon, but Merodach-baladan escaped from captivity, murdered him, and resumed the Babylonian crown, 131; burning with the desire of revenge Sennacherib hastened to Kisu, utterly routed the Babylonians, and Merodach-baladan fled for safety to the marshes, 131, 132; Babylon and the neighbouring cities were plundered, and hundreds of villages destroyed, 132; Bel-ibni, a court favourite, was placed on the throne, the Nomad tribes were severely punished, and 208,000 prisoners, with their cattle, carried away to Assyria; a force was also left to watch for Merodach-baladan, who collected his adherents and abandoned his country; founded a Chaldæan colony in Elam, 133, 134; Suzub next defied Sennacherib's power, but was defeated, and fled for safety to the swamps; Bel-ibni deposed, and Assur-nadin-mu set up as king in his stead, 134; a powerful expedition sent by sea against the new colony, landed, defeated them and their allies, and forced large numbers with the cattle into the ships, and conveyed them to Bab-salimiti, 134–37; Babylon captured in the interim by the Chaldæans and Elamites, and Suzub again proclaimed king, but defeated by the Assyrian reinforcements and taken captive, sent bound to Nineveh; a large army ravaged Elam with fire and sword, and destroyed most of the large cities; Suzub escaped from confinement, revolted, and at first sought safety in the marshes, and afterwards in Elam, where he raised a considerable army, returned to Babylon, mounted the throne, and expelled the Assyrians from the country, 137–9; the assistance of the Elamites was obtained by Suzub with the treasures of Bel, Nebo, and Nergal, sent as a present to Umman-minan, 140; Sennacherib eagerly met the rebels at Halule, where he gained a decisive victory, taking an incredible number of prisoners, and heaps of spoil, but retired on the approach of winter, 140, 141; the next year Babylon was stormed, given up to plunder, the images of the gods broken up, the city burnt and levelled with the ground, and Suzub, with part of his family, captured, 141, 142.

Shalmaneser III., sent three expeditions to Ituha, 115.

Simti-silhak, father of Kudur-mabuk, 80.

Sin-tabni-uzur, son of Ningal-idina, 151.

Suzub, see latter part of Sennacherib's wars, &c., 134–42.

TABLETS relating to the close of the Assyrian monarchy, 156, 157, n.

Tammaritu, an Elamite parricide, surrendered to Assur-bani-pal on a promise of pardon, 152, 153.

Teredon, a port on the Persian Gulf, 14.

Tiglath-pileser subdued several Babylonian tribes, appointed military governors, built Kar-Assur, and peopled it with captives; captured Nabu-usabsi, and impaled him in front of his capital, carrying off his wife, children, and gods, and a vast number of prisoners, 117, 118; took and sent Zakhiru captive to Assyria, but was foiled in the siege of Sapiya, and ravaged the surrounding country, 118, 119; proclaimed king of Babylon, and instituted festivals to the great gods in the principal cities, 119, 120.

Tower of Babel, notices of, 53, n.

Tugulti-Ninip, son of Shalmaneser, annexed Babylonia, and took the titles of "King of Assyria," "Conqueror of Karduniyas," and "King of Sumir and Akkad," but the Babylonians regained their independence shortly after his death, 94, 95.

ULBAR-SARKI-IDINA succeeded by his two brothers, 104, 105.

Umman-Aldas, king of Elam, murdered by his brothers, Urtaki and Te-umman, for refusing to make war on Esar-haddon, when the former assumed the crown, but did not follow his own previous policy, 147.

Umman-Aldas, an Elamite commander, killed Inda-bigas, and

mounted the throne; gave up the dead body of Nabu-bel-zikri and the head of his armour-bearer to Assur-bani-pal's envoys, 154.

Umman-igas, bribed by Saul-mugina to join the confederacy against the Assyrians, sent his army to Babylon, when his son, Tammaritu, rebelled, defeated the royal troops, and sent his head as a present to Assur-bani-pal, and assumed the crown of Elam, 151, 152.

Ur (Mugheir) succeeded Nipur as the capital of South Chaldæa, 69, 70; outside the walls filled with graves of all ages; probably the birth-place of Abraham; devoted to the worship of the moon-god, 71; first ruler, perhaps, Lig-Bagas, 72, n.; high state of its arts, learning, and civilization; carving, cylindrical seals, inscriptions; language generally Semitic, but Accadian still used; religion highly poetic with respect to rank, descent, and local character of deities, 73, 74; the great gods, Anu, Bel, and Hea, 74.

Ur-hamsi cures Izdubar, 61.

Urtaki, king of Elam, joined Bel-basa, and some petty chiefs in a plundering expedition into Babylonia, which alarmed Saul-mugina, 148, 149; the Elamites were pursued whilst retreating with the spoil, routed, and driven across the frontiers by Assur-bani-pal, who soon afterwards conquered the country, and placed Umman-igas on the throne as a tributary, 149.

WINGED monster slain by Izdubar and Heabani, 57.

XISITHRUS, XISUTHRUS, HASIS-ADRA, the Babylonian Noah, 38, n.; residence, 53.

ZABU, the builder of the temples of Samas and Anunit at Sippara, 83.

Zamama-zikir-idina unable to repress the raids of the Elamites and Assyrians, 100, 101.

PUBLICATIONS

OF THE

SOCIETY FOR PROMOTING CHRISTIAN KNOWLEDGE.

Early Britain.

A Series of Books which has for its aim the presentation of Early Britain at great historic periods.

ANGLO-SAXON BRITAIN. By GRANT ALLEN, B.A. With Map. Fcap. 8vo., cloth boards, 2s. 6d.

CELTIC BRITAIN. By Professor RHYS. With 2 Maps. Fcap. 8vo., cloth boards, 3s.

NORMAN BRITAIN. By the Rev. W. Hunt. With Map. Fcap. 8vo., cloth boards, 2s. 6d.

ROMAN BRITAIN. By the Rev. Prebendary SCARTH. With Map. Fcap. 8vo., cloth boards, 2s. 6d.

Non-Christian Religious Systems.

Fcap. 8vo., Cloth boards, price 2s. 6d. each.

BUDDHISM. Being a Sketch of the Life and Teachings of Gautama, the Buddha. By T. W. RHYS DAVIDS, of the Middle Temple. With Map.

BUDDHISM IN CHINA. By the Rev. S. BEAL. With Map.

CONFUCIANISM AND TAOUISM. By Professor ROBERT K. DOUGLAS, of the British Museum. With Map.

CORÂN (THE): its Composition and Teaching, and the Testimony it bears to the Holy Scriptures. By Sir WILLIAM MUIR, K.C.S.I., LL.D.

HINDUISM. By MONIER WILLIAMS, M.A., D.C.L., &c. With Map.

ISLAM AND ITS FOUNDER. By J. W. H. STOBART, B.A., Principal, La Martinière College, Lucknow. With Map.

Diocesan Histories.

This Series, which will embrace, when completed, every Diocese in England and Wales, will furnish, it is expected, a perfect library of English Ecclesiastical History.

CANTERBURY. By the Rev. R. C. JENKINS. With Map. Fcap. 8vo., cloth boards, 3s. 6d.

CHICHESTER. By the Rev. W. R. W. STEPHENS. With Map and Plan. Fcap. 8vo., cloth boards, 2s. 6d.

DURHAM. By the Rev. J. L. LOW. With Map and Plan. Fcap. 8vo., cloth boards, 2s. 6d.

LICHFIELD. By the Rev. W. BERESFORD. With Map. Fcap. 8vo., cloth boards, 2s. 6d.

NORWICH. By the Rev. A. JESSOPP, D.D. With Map. Fcap. 8vo., cloth boards, 2s. 6d.

OXFORD. By the Rev. E. MARSHALL, M.A. With Map. Fcap. 8vo., cloth boards, 2s. 6d.

PETERBOROUGH. By the Rev. G. A. POOLE, M.A. With Map. Fcap. 8vo., cloth boards, 2s. 6d.

SALISBURY. By the Rev. W. H. JONES. With Map and Plan. Fcap. 8vo., cloth boards, 2s. 6d.

WINCHESTER. By the Rev. W. BENHAM, B.D. With Map. Fcap. 8vo., cloth boards, 2s. 6d.

WORCESTER. By the Rev. I. GREGORY SMITH, M.A., and the Rev. PHIPPS ONSLOW, M.A. With Map. Fcap. 8vo., cloth boards, 3s. 6d.

YORK. By the Rev. Canon ORNSBY, M.A. With Map. Fcap. 8vo., cloth boards, 3s. 6d.

LONDON:
NORTHUMBERLAND AVENUE, CHARING CROSS, W.C.;
43, QUEEN VICTORIA STREET, E.C.
26, ST. GEORGE'S PLACE, HYDE PARK CORNER, S.W.
BRIGHTON: 135, NORTH STREET.

Ingram Content Group UK Ltd.
Milton Keynes UK
UKHW012256280623
424184UK00007B/426

9 781018 452340